the
ENLIGHTENMENT
PROJECT

carrie triffet

gentle
joyous
INDUSTRIES

Gentle Joyous Industries
3875-A Telegraph Road #218
Ventura, CA 93003
www.gentlejoyous.com

ISBN 10: 0-9838421-1-6
ISBN 13: 978-0-9838421-1-8

Library of Congress Control Number: 2011934585
Printed in the United States of America

Book Design: Carrie Triffet
Author photos: Isabel Lawrence Photographers
www.isabellawrence.com

CONTENTS

PART ONE
objects in mirror are closer than they appear

CHAPTER ONE
oneness and the ego mind

The road less traveled	16
I could be wrong	17
Got sanity?	21
The ego mind	25
The prodigal child, circa 1967	27

CHAPTER TWO
speaking of enlightenment

Paradoxes on the road to enlightenment	34
Multiple kinds of Oneness	39
Spiritual awakening	41
Degrees of awakening	44
So what is enlightenment, exactly?	46
Enlightenment versus awakening	49

CHAPTER THREE
hysterical blindness

Bits and pieces	54
The dinner table awakening	62
The ego as enemy – Part I	65
Can enlightenment rub off?	67
Expedient means	72

CHAPTER FOUR
the serious beginning

Question everything	76
Trust, faith and belief – Part I	79
(en)Lighten up!	84
Trust, faith and belief – Part II	85
Faith versus blind faith	87
How can I tell if I'm doing it right?	89
If I'm enlightened, can I still be wrong?	91

CHAPTER FIVE
down to earth

Chasing your bliss	94
Letting go	97
In the world? Or *of* the world? – Part I	102
The dinner party	105

PART TWO
I'll stop the world and melt with you

CHAPTER SIX
vision correction as a daily practice

Where the rubber meets the road	111
The body as truth meter	114
In the world? Or *of* the world? – Part II	116
Self-inquiry – Part I	118
That's entertainment	119

CHAPTER SEVEN
forgiveness and joining

Forgiveness	122
Joining	135
The basics of joining	138
Joining with another person	139
Joining with Spirit	140
The joining pool	141
The joining pool as a micro-meditation	143
Joining the Oneness within	145
Oneness meets Oneness	145
Joining with the void	147
The ego as enemy – Part II	149
Night of the end of days	153

CHAPTER EIGHT
judgment and stories

Judgment and the power of belief	158
The link between non-judgment and Oneness	162
Connecting the dots	164
When ego masquerades as Spirit	170
Crashing the gateless gate	172

CHAPTER NINE
enemy mine

The projector, the projection and British Petroleum	176
Joining with the filmstrip	180
In the world? Or *of* the world? – Part III: On battling illness	186
Self-inquiry – Part II	188
Self-inquiry combined with joining pool meditation	190
The devil you know	193

CHAPTER TEN
other supplemental practices

Mind mastery	196
Observing the mind	197
No-mind meditation	201
Being in the now	202
Non-resistance	204

CHAPTER ELEVEN
manifestation and oneness

The attractive law of attraction 210

Law of attraction basics 212

Feeling becomes fact 214

Mind mastery – Part II 216

It's now or never 220

Postscript: Lord willing (and the creek don't rise) 230

Afterchat with Nouk Sanchez: The miracle of surrender 239

PART ONE

objects in mirror
are closer
than they appear

CHAPTER ONE

oneness
and the ego mind

THE ROAD LESS TRAVELED

If enlightenment were a country—let's call it the United State of Oneness—and we were planning a trip there on our next vacation, it would be a good idea to read up on the place beforehand. Get the lay of the land.

(I know, I know, enlightenment isn't a destination, and we can't get there from here. Bear with me, please. It's an analogy.)

The moment we cracked open the first enlightenment brochure or attended the first lecture, we would discover its language and customs are incomprehensible to those of us who don't already live there. The place is just too different from our own. We would need some kind of translator or guide, just to help us start making sense of the guidebook.

That, hopefully, is where this book comes in.

I don't live in that mythical country, but I have visited now and then. I'm not a native speaker by any means, but I well understand the needs of a traveler en route to this strange land. I can do my best to translate for you. Maybe help you find a public restroom, or hail a cab. I've also been given a pretty great set of maps; they're well tested, and they've never failed me. I can share them with you, if you like. You might find them useful along the way.

My own impressions of this strange country are fleeting, so they're naturally spotty and incomplete. I'm not the most experienced guide, God knows. But if you're interested, I'll let you in on everything I've learned so far on my own journey.

I COULD BE WRONG

A Course in Miracles famously asks: Would you rather be right or happy?

Everybody understands this deceptively simple question to some degree, and anybody—spiritually inclined or not—can answer it.

For the first few decades of my life, I would have confidently answered *I want to be right, of course.* That's because I thought happiness was for people who weren't smart enough to notice how screwed up the world was. And since I was convinced legitimate happiness didn't exist, smug superiority was my consolation prize of choice.

It was only after ten or fifteen years of sincere spiritual practice that I began to realize my habitual cynicism wasn't fun anymore; being right was actually causing me pain. Maybe it was time to give happy another look.

Yet this understanding of the "right or happy" equation barely scratched the surface of its true meaning. As any sincere student of Oneness can tell you, there's quite a lot more riding on your answer than initially meets the eye.

This is what that question is really asking: Do you want to remain a slave to your fixed belief in this illusory world, causing yourself unimaginable pain in the process? Or do you want to discard what you think you know, and see the perfect, joyous truth as it really is?

You might still think it sounds like a no-brainer. *Oh, that's an easy one*, you say to yourself. *If being right is the source of all pain and illusion, and choosing happiness would bring perfect truth and joy, then I definitely vote for happy.*

"Right or happy" may seem an obvious question, maybe even a little bit glib. Yet it's not a glib or obvious or easy question. The choice between right and happy is pretty much the deepest, toughest question ever asked of anyone, and inside that question's honest answer is found the very heart of enlightenment.

Oh, and the destruction of everything you've ever known.

•   •   •

Yes, welcome to Oneness. If you're anything like me, it's probably more than you initially signed up for. At first glance, enlightenment seems like such a gentle pursuit, after all; a sweetly peaceful pastime for the most serene among us.

Not.

Nothing could be further from the truth, in fact. Enlightenment is the most radical aspiration known to mankind, because choosing the path of enlightenment is the end of all certainty. Once you've authentically voted for happy, this fact remains: To abandon your addiction to certainty—to being right—is the dismantling of your world as you know it.

Anyway, that's what I'm personally all about these days; I'm in a heavy-duty dismantling phase. If you'd have asked me three years ago, or five years ago, if I was serious about wanting to be enlightened, I'd have said, *Hell yes, I'm serious.*

But I wasn't. Not really.

That's because it takes a sincere desire for the truth at all costs, and although I was mighty fond of the truth, I wasn't willing to trade my entire world for it.

But now I am. Enlightenment or bust.

And so I've begun to sincerely question everything I think I know, and take nobody's secondhand word for anything. I'm not particularly anarchic by nature, so all this questioning of the status quo doesn't come naturally or easily. In fact, there's been quite a lot of *who the hell do I think I am?* every time I refuse to take the word of a great scholar or sage or political figure at face value.

Firsthand experience is the only useful touchstone in this process of kicking the addiction to certainty. So I'm groping my way in the dark, going only by what feels authentic based on my own direct experience. And I'm chucking the rest.

This is the start of the necessary dismantling process, and it's as spooky as it sounds. But after all these years of only pretending to be serious about enlightenment, I'm relieved to have finally begun.

How did I get this way, you ask? I'm not entirely sure. This dismantling phase, and this book, have both been welling up spontaneously from someplace deep within me. Uncomfortable as it's been, I still wouldn't trade the experience for anything. This is my enlightenment project, and in writing down my findings along the way, it's my hope that you, too, can find something in these pages to help you with your own awakening process.

Having said that, however, I'd like to stress this point: In our world of shifting viewpoints and extenuating circumstances, there's no such thing as one-size-fits-all truth. We each perceive the world differently, and what works for me may not work quite the same way for you. Even though everything I describe or recommend in these pages is Spirit-inspired, it's all based solely on my own personal experience. This is my truth, but I don't automatically assume it's your truth, too.

Most spiritual teachings and teachers seem to miss this point. In their excitement to have found a teaching or method that works, they joyfully proclaim, "This is the way!" But it isn't really. It's *a* way. One of many, many ways. And their way will be a good fit for some, but not others.

So, explore the teachings you feel drawn to. Take it all in. And then move forward according to your own personal experience and no one else's. You're the only one who matters, on your own personal journey toward happy. Seriously. Do what feels authentic for *you*.

GOT SANITY?

As any serious student of Oneness will tell you, this world is not real. In reality, all things are One, and that One has no measurable characteristics of any kind. Each of us is an intrinsic part of the One, along with everything that's ever been or ever will be. The One goes by lots of different names, depending on the background of the student, but its characteristics are always the same.

The One merely is. Eternally. And this eternal Oneness is the truth of all existence.

So if everything is One, where does that leave *this* world? According to Oneness, anything with weight or mass or energy can't be real: *No measurable characteristics* means just that. If you can touch it, see it, hear it or taste it, it's not real. If it produces heat or energy, it's not real. If it takes up space, it isn't real.

Nothing separate from the One can be real. And nothing can occur here or there, yesterday or tomorrow—because in eternity, time doesn't exist and there's no such thing as space.

In short, nothing at all in our 3-D universe of form is real.

To sum up: We see things that aren't real and believe in things that aren't true. Objectively speaking, this evidence would strongly suggest we're all insane.

Yet it doesn't seem that way to us, because, well, if we're *all* insane, then insanity looks pretty normal, doesn't it? After all, everybody's doing it. Of course, some people seem to operate way beyond the bounds of what we collectively consider normal behavior, so we label those people insane.

We judge insanity—along with everything else—on a sliding scale. But that scale looks a little bit different to each of us, depending on our own unique perception and experiences.

For instance, I might be tempted to judge the makers of the *Jackass* movies and TV shows a little bit more insane than most. These films are, in the words of one critic, "filled with the sort of suicidal stunts parental warnings were invented for." (For a taste of the kind of insanity *Jackass* favors, I give you two words: Rocket skates.)

On the other hand, if the *Jackass* crew were to hear me say, "This world is not real," chances are they'd make exactly the same judgment about me: *That lady is off her rocker.*

Yardsticks and sliding scales, then, are useless. In this world, insanity is in the eye of the beholder.

• • •

Our own ego minds block the truth of all reality. We prefer to see only this 3-D fantasy world instead, which displays characteristics that are opposite those of eternal Oneness. In Oneness, there is One truth that's always equally true, no matter how you look at it. There are no extenuating circumstances that could ever make it less true, because the truth of Oneness is changeless and eternal and complete. And because eternal truth never changes, perfect certainty and safety are found within it.

But this world, the one we call home, is one of sliding scales and relative truths. In our shifting, unstable 3-D world, nothing is eternal—least of all you and me. To protect our fragile selves from physical or emotional harm, we're perpetually on guard against outside attack. In this world, it's the survival of the fittest.

Isn't it?

That's what our ego minds tell us. But it's this very counsel—this "us versus them" view of the world—that is responsible for blocking ultimate truth. It's our crazy egoic perception that steers us wrong every time. To be released from the insane influence of our own ego minds, then, is to awaken to eternal truth.

There are a couple of ways to go about this.

You can wait around hoping you spontaneously awaken to the truth. That can definitely happen, and usually occurs once or twice in a generation. Which would give you roughly a one-in-three-and-a-half-billion chance it's going to be you.

I know what that approach is like; I used to operate on the hazy hope that I would someday be that one lucky individual. I diligently kept up my daily spiritual practice, all the while dreaming of the distant day enlightenment would suddenly happen to me and change my life forever. As if enlightenment were Prince Charming coming for me on a white steed. My only job, then, was to keep sweeping those embers every day, biding my time until I was presented with that glass slipper.

If that's the approach you want to take, there's nothing wrong with it. But if you're truly interested in awakening to the truth of Oneness, it seems to me you might be better off turning away from the passive dream of a happily ever after.

The more proactive option is to help the process along by actively working to restore your own sanity, gradually lessening the ego's influence on your mental functioning. I've tried both approaches, and I prefer the active one. I feel it's well worth the effort it takes to prepare myself for awakening, by helping to weaken my own reliance on faulty egoic perception.

Personally, I'd like to be strong enough to turn away from my ego's influence altogether as soon as I can manage it. I don't much like who I am, or how I feel, when I'm actively under the influence. This is because the ego mind has no foundation in truth, so it feels vulnerable to attack and constantly seeks to shore itself up. To protect itself, it forms alliances with other ego minds that agree with it, and attacks those that don't. This business of ever-shifting alliances means we all spend our lives teetering precariously, as if we're each balancing on a slippery plank perched atop a beach ball. I'd rather not operate that way anymore.

Oh, sure, some of us (the well-balanced ones) get the hang of it, more or less. We constantly adjust to life's slight changes, making the balancing act look easy.

Others are falling off all the time.

But either way, it's exhausting and unsafe for us all. And it's not how we're meant to live.

THE EGO MIND

Spirituality borrows—ok, steals—psychological terminology when it speaks of the ego mind. Yet the meaning is not precisely the same.

In psychology, the ego commonly refers to the conscious mind of a single individual. The term is often used interchangeably with the personality-self definition of "I" or "me." This definition of the ego doesn't include the unconscious mind, which is thought to occupy its own domain.

But in the spirituality of Oneness, the ego mind is considered way bigger than the single individual. It belongs jointly to *all* the single individuals.

According to some forms of Oneness, this is how the ego creation story goes: We used to know we were One infinite being. We also knew this state of Oneness was non-negotiable. We were One infinite mind, and that single truth was the only truth of all existence.

Yet we wanted to be separate individuals instead, so we chose to take a little detour from truth. We decided to manufacture an ego mind to help us accomplish this impossible task.

The ego mind is, by necessity, absolutely bonkers. It operates entirely independently from the only truth and the only reality there is. Its function is to block the One truth from our memory by showing us a constant stream of very convincing lies instead.

In the spiritual definition, the ego refers both to the collective false mind we all share (because there is only One of us in truth), and also to the false mind and false personality-self of each individual person. This ego definition includes not only the thinking mind, but also the deeply buried unconscious beliefs that fuel all ego minds, both the personal and the collective. The ego is not a separate entity—although we tend, for convenience's sake, to sometimes speak of it as if it is; it's an inextricable part of our One self that we collectively and individually use to hide from the truth.

The eternal truth has never gone away; it hasn't even changed a bit in all these eons we've been playing with separate identities. It waits in perfect peace for us to wake up and voluntarily choose reality as it truly is.

To (re)awaken to the truth of Oneness, then, all we need to do is reject the influence of both the personal and the collective ego mind, and choose eternal truth instead.

Hey, how hard could it be?

The collective ego mind is determined to keep the 3-D world in place, and on a deeply unconscious level, so are we all. But why are we so intent on resisting reality? Gary Renard's book, *The Disappearance of the Universe*, reinterprets the bible's prodigal son story as a way of explaining our mistaken motivation for hiding from eternal truth.

I've chosen to update this reinterpretation of the story to 1967—partly because it tickles me to dress the protagonist in love beads and paisley bell bottoms, but also because it gives me the opportunity to expand a bit on the original. Through this modernized parable, I can more thoroughly explore and explain some of the motivations behind our fierce resistance to the reality of Oneness. One last note: In this book, I don't typically traffic in biblical terminology. I make an exception for parts of this parable, because of its unavoidably God-centric worldview.

THE PRODIGAL CHILD, CIRCA 1967

Ok, let's say you are the only child of a single parent, the One who gave you life. You live within your creator's home, and you are its spitting image. A chip off the old block, as it were.

That's because you're made of the very same stuff as your creator. And because you're made of this same raw material as your creator, you possess all the same traits and powers, in the same full measure, as your creator. You are the One child of the One parent, and together you are still One. Call it the math of ultimate truth: Your creator creates constantly—always creating more of itself, out of the raw material of itself—and all its creations forever add up to One.

Nothing can ever change that fact. Your creator made the rules before you got here, and it's impossible to alter them in any way. So your permanent address is within your creator's home, and your changeless safety and limitless peace are a forever, non-negotiable fact, whether you like it or not.

One day, you decide you're tired of being One, because although you're perfect, you're not special. There's nothing about you that stands out in any way from the rest of perfection, which is whole and complete. So you begin to formulate a radical new idea: Maybe you'll invent some imaginary friends to play with for a change. *Perfect Oneness is great*, you think, *but wouldn't it be interesting to see how I measure up against somebody else? Who knows, maybe I'm even more perfect than my pretend friends. Or less perfect. How will I find out unless I try it?*

You know your imaginary friends can't be real, since the very idea of them violates the immutable laws of your creator's home. There's only perfect sameness in the One self, with creator and created forever united. No part of One can be different or better or worse than any other part. So you're afraid your creator might get really angry, if it finds out you're thinking about breaking those unbreakable rules. And yet you want to do it anyway.

You decide you need some privacy away from loving eyes. Your solution is to build your own little imaginary room within your creator's house. It's the coolest room ever: Purple shag carpeting on the floor and black light posters on the walls. You throw a party to show off your new place, inviting all your imaginary friends over. Then you light some incense, put on a Jimi Hendrix record and you all drop acid together.

Only it's a far more powerful drug than you bargained for, and it makes you forget you were pretending. The imaginary friends all seem real to you now, and the little room has become an inescapable prison. Your hallucinations are punctuated by scattered moments of beauty and fun, but mostly this trip is filled with terrible nightmare images that are completely unlike the magnificent life you're used to.

Think about it: Before you made these separate friends, you were One. You were in permanent communion with your One self; you always knew what was on your (changelessly perfect) collective mind. But now, each of you has a separate mind, and each mind harbors a different agenda. You don't know what they're thinking. You're no longer safe. It isn't just the drug making you paranoid; you have good reason to be scared and deeply mistrustful of these "others."

You're very confused and desperately fearful now: Afraid of those real-seeming friends, afraid of this awful new place, afraid of your own unpredictable power—after all you unexpectedly created this crazy new universe of form, just by wishing for it. You thought it'd be nice to dabble in separateness, and *this* is what you got. Talk about the law of unintended consequences!

Yes, you've found plenty to be afraid of in your little private room. But above all, you're afraid your creator will find out and give you hell (literally) for what you've done.

After all, you've squandered your inheritance.

In the original version of the prodigal son story, that inheritance is described as financial wealth; it is generally assumed, therefore, that the fortune in question is composed of actual money. Piles and piles of canvas bags with dollar signs on them, stashed away in a vault somewhere, like some kind of Scrooge McDuck cartoon.

Think again. Your inheritance is eternal safety and divine peace. Your inheritance is the ability to create constantly in the same joyful way your creator creates.

But what have you been creating? Not safety or joy or peace. No, you've been creating pretend rooms filled with terrifying strangers partaking of purple haze and *Purple Haze*. Man, are you ever in trouble.

What you've forgotten in your drug-addled state is that your One loving parent knows everything. (Your creator is *you*, remember?) After all, your locked room, your privacy, the acid and all those scary frenemies aren't truly real. How could they be?

Your One creator knows you're safe at home as you always were, and it waits patiently for you to snap out of this hallucination. Your creator doesn't judge anything you're doing as bad or sinful. "Bad" and "sinful" are concepts that don't exist in the always-loving house of the One who gave you life.

In the original prodigal son story, after many years of suffering on his own, the son realizes he wants to go home to his Father's house—even if it means being punished for all his transgressions.

Upon his return he discovers, of course, that his Father extends only love and welcome to him.

And this is the true point of the story, according to *The Disappearance of the Universe*. Our deep, unconscious fear of God serves no purpose. In truth we've done nothing wrong, and no punishment awaits us in the eternally welcoming home of our creator.

We find that impossible to believe, you and I.

After all, we accidentally on purpose tore Heaven apart. If the roles were reversed *we* wouldn't forgive us.

And, thanks to our "us versus them" egoic perception, we *don't* forgive us. In our estimation we've sinned on a colossal scale, and we don't dare return home for fear of the punishment that surely awaits us. Yet our One creator knows we're perfect and blameless. A return to Oneness brings no punishment—only sanity and safety and peace.

But maybe you're not yet interested in leaving your private room behind? There are some awfully interesting and entertaining things to occupy you in there. Staying awhile longer might seem like a lot more fun than rejoining with your creator.

Or maybe you are interested in going home, but you're still afraid the price of rejoining would be way too high. Don't worry, that's just the drug talking. Either way, there's no pressure on any of us.

Your One creator loves you completely, and it would never choose something for you that you haven't yet chosen for yourself. Like the prodigal son story, it waits patiently until you decide to come home of your own free will. It will offer you constant help along the way, should you want it, but the choices you make are always your own.

You are powerful enough (omnipotent creator, you) to shrug off the effects of the drug and go home anytime you want. You just need to want it with all parts of your mind united. With One-mindedness, in other words.

When your mind chooses wholeness and you authentically want your sanity back, the drug will leave your system and you will remember there's never been a barrier between yourself and your Self. You were only pretending all along.

And, just as in the original version of the story, you will discover your One creator is overjoyed to have you back in the place you never left.

CHAPTER TWO

speaking
of enlightenment

I guess I should say this right upfront: It's impossible to talk accurately about enlightenment. To speak of enlightenment is to grasp at something that can't be pinned down, with a tool wholly unsuited to the job. It's like trying to capture the memory of how a ripe peach smells, using a butterfly net.

And yet, here I am, net in hand, giving it my best shot anyway. With this in mind, it seems as good a time as any to bring up the following topic.

PARADOXES ON THE ROAD TO ENLIGHTENMENT

The first of these is that there's no "road" to enlightenment.

"You're already "there," so there's nowhere to go," says that book by that very enlightened guy. "The moment you start trying to "get" somewhere on the road to nowhere, you've lost your way.

Why? Because all goals and all desires are products of the ego mind. And the ego mind can never become enlightened. There can be no getting, no striving, no "becoming" enlightened. Enlightenment merely is."

I don't know about you, but whenever I used to hear enlightened people talking this way I got frustrated as hell. *Is it absolutely necessary to speak in annoying circular riddles about enlightenment?* I would wonder.

Well—yes and no.

Yes, because direct spiritual experience is totally unlike anything we can relate to in this world, and entirely beyond the scope of human language to express. Trust me, I've done my best to describe the indescribable. I've experienced brief moments of pure Oneness with the divine; I refer to these as powerful awakenings, because that's what they felt like. My life was forever changed after the first of these in 2005. I wrote about that experience in my first book, and could only manage to speak of it in metaphor. Direct description was impossible.

So I can imagine the experience of living permanently in an awakened state (AKA enlightenment, or self-realization) would be virtually impossible to communicate, because it is completely unlike anything we know. There are no points of reference, and no way to describe what it is—only what it isn't.

And descriptions of what it *isn't* somehow are never quite what the rest of us are hoping to hear: Enlightenment isn't a destination to get to, and there's no road to get there. And there's no point in striving to arrive, since we're already there.

(Well, thanks for your help, Enlightened Guy. To say we're already there may be technically accurate, but it's a fairly useless piece of information for those of us who aren't yet awake to that reality.)

Ok, so there's no striving, no place and no road. There's also no goal of future enlightenment to look forward to, because past and future aren't real; we can only choose to awaken to Oneness in the now. Reality, after all, is the eternal now moment. And all goals are meaningless because we already are that thing we seek to become.

So you can see why it's maddeningly difficult to talk accurately about this stuff.

•　　　•　　　•

Yet even beyond the difficulties of speaking about it, the built-in conundrums are even trickier where enlightenment is involved. For instance, while it's true that you can't "set a goal" or "strive" for enlightenment and hope to attain it (since both of those activities guarantee you'll never "get there"), in my experience goals and striving are necessary anyway. At least for a while.

This is what I mean by that: Your ego mind doesn't give away its real estate willingly. It has a great deal invested in keeping things exactly as they are. Your ego wants you to go on believing in its version of the world for as long as possible. It very much wants you to attack and defend; it wants you to keep judging and seeing everybody and everything as separate from yourself, with all parts having separate agendas and different interests from your own.

It wants you to think of yourself as a unique individual. But your personality-self—all your likes and dislikes, your talents and limitations; everything you think of as who you are—isn't real. It's your belief in the reality of your own personality-self that guarantees your ego its permanent job security. Stated another way, your belief in the reality of your personality-self is the only thing keeping your individual identity (and therefore your ego mind) alive.

In Oneness, individual personality-selves have no function, no purpose. In perfect divine sameness there can be no such thing as individuality. So if you were to decide you're tired of living a fantasy life that keeps you from ever remembering divine truth, you would need only choose to remember Oneness instead. And in doing so, your attachment to individuality would be released, allowing you to awaken to the world as it really is.

And that awakening could theoretically happen in an instant. Any instant would do; the truth goes on unceasingly and unchangingly, whether we're aware of it or not. But the moment we're one hundred percent awake and fully accepting the truth of all existence, the ego mind would be out of a job.

Since it isn't real, the ego's only choice would then be to dissolve away into nothingness. And way deep down, your ego mind knows it, even if you're not consciously aware of this fact.

In my opinion it's necessary (at least for a while) to have

a "goal" of enlightenment, because I find it absolutely does take conscious effort. You'll likely encounter a lot of internal resistance when you first try to contradict the ego's interpretation of the world, and side instead with the truth of Oneness. It will probably be uncomfortable.

After all, we're hardwired to see flaws and guilt everywhere we look—judgment is our ego's favorite tool for keeping us invested in separation. To learn to consistently look beyond the ego mind's habitual assumptions takes time and willingness and work.

This is the practice of retraining our minds to accept the incomparable perfection that we really are. It's not easy. It runs counter to everything we think we know about ourselves and the world in which we live. And without a goal to get us through these first unfamiliar stages, it's doubtful anybody would keep going.

For awhile, then, goals and striving remain useful to us. The farther we get along the "road" to enlightenment, the more we need to abandon the reassuring blacks and whites in our worldview. We start having to embrace the grays: Yes, we accept that goals are created and sustained entirely by the ego mind—yet we also accept that we have need of goals for awhile. And that's the funny thing about awakening; contradictory truths start to coexist all over the place. "Either/or" no longer works nearly as well as it used to.

The thing to keep an eye on while engaged in the business of striving for enlightenment, is any tendency to become frustrated or impatient about the perceived pace of progress (or lack thereof).

These are understandable reactions, but it's important to guard against them. They're of no use to you, and will only slow you down. All forms of dissatisfaction are products of the ego mind. If dissatisfaction with life in the false 3-D world has caused you to form a goal of waking up to remember the truth of Oneness, so be it. Do your best to be at peace with that conundrum. But dissatisfaction that you're not "getting there" as quickly as you'd like will never help.

We'll encounter plenty more paradoxes like this one, on our rocky road trip. For now, let's just say Oneness is a spiritual path in which we learn to accept the paradoxes and keep "moving forward" anyway. Even though there's no place to get to. Even though we're already there.

MULTIPLE KINDS OF ONENESS

Like everything else here in the unreliable land of 3-D, we find lots of seemingly conflicting firsthand descriptions of the enlightened state. This makes sense, because even though enlightenment is an awakening to Oneness, each of us perceives everything—even Oneness—a bit differently from everybody else.

Many of these firsthand descriptions identify Oneness as the simple realization that we are not separate from all that is. This type of description tends not to include transcendent joy or ecstatic union; some of them do not make any mention of love, divine or otherwise. They just say enlightenment is waking up to the fact that separation isn't real, period. All is One.

This is where I'm coming from: *A Course in Miracles* speaks of four overlapping "stages" of awakening. The first of these is Dualism, which is the unquestioned belief in separation and the reality of the 3-D world; it's where we all start out.

The second stage is Semi-Dualism, a condition that vacillates unpredictably between belief and disbelief in separation, according to the circumstances at hand.

The third stage would be Non-Dualism, otherwise known as the realization of Oneness. It is this state that seems to be the one most often described by enlightened people when they write or speak about their own enlightenment. This is the state I have visited on occasion, and just as the enlightened guys tend to describe it, I found no joy or bliss in it. I felt only a deep sense of peace in the absence of separation.

The *Course*, however, describes a fourth stage of awakening known as Pure Non-Dualism. This one would become available only after the mind was completely free of illusion and able to fully embrace the truth. This total lack of resistance to the truth would allow the healed mind to be reclaimed by the infinite One mind. This reunion with the creator is the state that is described as embodying—among other things—limitless joy and perfect divine love.

Because I'm questioning everything in my world, I've had to extend my practice of self-inquiry even into this previously sacrosanct subject matter. I've had to question whether I know for a fact that this fourth stage is real. And the answer is this: Much as I'd like to, I can't yet personally verify the existence of Pure Non-Dualism.

On the other hand, I can't dismiss it, either. Spirit has repeatedly shown me glimpses of a state that would seem to embody the attributes of Pure Non-Dualism. It has also spoken to me many times of the divine love and infinite joy that are to be found as truth is embraced fully.

When I speak about enlightenment in this book, I'm mainly talking about the third stage of Non-Dualism. That's because it's the one that's next on my list. But in my heart, I'm holding open a spot for stage four out of four. Just in case it really does exist.

SPIRITUAL AWAKENING

They call it awakening because once you start to awaken, you feel as if you've spent your whole life sleepwalking through a powerfully persuasive dream state—and that's because you have. You've been sound asleep within the dream of separation that is concocted and held in place by your ego mind.

This ongoing dream that we call "the world" has no reality; it only seems real because of the ego belief we continually invest and reinvest in it. Although it may not seem like it, we're all here entirely by choice; together we willingly sustain the illusion of the 3-D world from moment to moment. Theoretically, every single moment offers a fresh opportunity to withdraw this ego belief and awaken from the dream. Yet we habitually choose the dream instead.

On a largely unconscious level we've all agreed to stand in line, as it were, clutching our tickets for yet another ride on the rollercoaster. Like it or not, it's a thoroughly voluntary amusement park.

•   •   •

This is one simple way to describe the ego mind: It's the part of the mind that resists what is. The ego is never at peace. It's always pushing away what it doesn't want or yearning for what it does want; that's how it functions. This constant pursuing and rejecting is what gives us our separate sense of self, our tastes and preferences that make us uniquely different from everyone and everything around us. *I like this, I don't like that. I need this in order to be happy. I could do with a whole lot less of that.* This is how our stories get written. We ourselves created the ego mind for precisely this purpose.

A minute ago I said the ego mind is never at peace—that it can never be satisfied. Does that strike you as an unfair overstatement? 'Never' is a harsh concept, after all. Maybe you feel there are times in your life when you've been truly and completely satisfied. If this is the case, I would suggest it makes for an excellent self-inquiry question: *Am I really completely content? Or do I just tell myself that I am?*

Sure, it's a potentially scary line of questioning. Don't say I didn't warn you. But I assure you, I'm not setting off firecrackers inside your house just for the hell of it. I bring up this subject with good reason. It's important that we look carefully, to see what our ego minds (and therefore our stories) are really made of.

Why do I say our ego minds can never be truly satisfied? The ego, left to its own devices, is incapable of single-mindedness— One-mindedness—because it was designed to block out that very thing. To see with all parts of the mind united would actually be quite dangerous to the ego; its very existence would be at risk. So the ego never perceives anything in a way that's fully stable or fully united.

I'll give you an example of what I mean: Let's say you are fortunate enough to have a fulfilling career, a loving family, a beautiful home. It's everything you ever dreamed of. As you look around at all the treasures in your life, you feel completely satisfied.

But do you really? Maybe you occasionally feel a little stab of fear that this good fortune won't last. Or a faint suspicion you're not worthy of it. Maybe even a small intermittent longing for those days when you were young and single with fewer responsibilities. Not that you'd trade your current happiness for it, of course—but you and your friends sure did have fun back in those carefree days...

And this is how ego minds operate. By telling ourselves stories of fear, shame or longing, we guarantee that true peace remains impossible.

Anyway, back to awakening. You start to wake up, and as you metaphorically rub those sleepy eyes and squint at your surroundings, you begin to realize the person you think of as "yourself" isn't really who you are. *Yourself* is just a complex fantasy composed of your own conflicted ideas, beliefs and stories you've made up about you and your relationship to the world. None of it actually exists.

Once you start to awaken, once those metaphorical eyelids start to flutter open, the whole fake ego world of stories and beliefs starts to crumble. Your sense of self is found nowhere other than within the stories you've made up, or accepted about the world. Those stories and your personal identity are not just connected; they're actually the same thing.

To awaken to any degree is to realize—permanently, or sometimes for just a fleeting second—that you're not the individual person you thought you were, living inside a body and bound by laws of time and space. You realize you are none of those things. You're everyone and you're everything. And no one and nothing. You're simultaneously everywhere and nowhere, eternally. You *are* eternity itself.

Oh sure, it might sound great on paper, but it can actually be a pretty freaky thing while it's happening. So much so, that you could choose to snap right back into your old, limited sense of self as soon as that awakening experience is over. But trust me, you'll never be quite the same again afterward. With that first brief glimpse of reality, your world of stories has already begun to collapse.

DEGREES OF AWAKENING

I describe my first awakening experience as life-changing, and it certainly was. Looking back, I think of my life pre-awakening as one existence, and the one post-awakening as another. Yet the experience itself lasted for less than a minute, as far as I can tell. Time ceased to exist, so it's hard to be absolutely sure how long it went on. Not like it matters.

Anyway, while it was occurring, I consciously chose against a real or permanent awakening. (I'll tell you more about that decision later.) But even if I'd chosen to awaken permanently—to be enlightened, in other words—I'm starting to realize it would've only been the beginning of my journey, not the end.

A big, flashy *OMG!* realization like my first one definitely will start the enlightenment ball rolling. And a permanent awakening means we'd consciously choose to stay awake afterward and remember everything we realized. But even during a permanent awakening, I suspect the amount of truth we internalize depends on how much resistance the ego mind is dishing out at the time.

A very strong ego will probably be able to push back hard, even during a permanent awakening. And that means some, but not all, of the One truth will be accepted. Which is to say, there's still work to do. Even after enlightenment, there may be levels and degrees of awakeness, resulting in only partial acceptance, healing and surrender.

Total awakening would be to accept and embrace the full truth of Oneness as an ongoing experience of life. To bring all unconscious resistance into the light. To be perfectly unified with reality, seeing with such purified eyesight that we're able to perceive all of life with the same vision as Spirit, in other words.

That would be awesome. That would bring us within spitting distance of that fourth stage of four.

Total awakening is available to all of us, by the way. It's not special—in fact it's the opposite of special. To be totally awake is nothing more than remembering and accepting what we already are. But hearing that doesn't make it any easier to accomplish, does it?

SO WHAT IS ENLIGHTENMENT, EXACTLY?

It's natural to want a clear definition of enlightenment that we can all understand. That way, we'll know what it is we're aiming for, right?

Well, good luck with that; I certainly can't help you, much as I might like to. I know just enough about the nature of enlightenment to realize it turns out I don't know anything at all. So if I were to be interviewed about this topic, this is more or less how it would go:

Q: What is enlightenment?

A: I have no idea.

And that would pretty much be the end of the interview.

See, this is the predicament in which we find ourselves: We can outline the various degrees and stages of enlightenment; we can even take a stab at describing a few of its attributes. But an ego mind can't hope to authentically know, let alone explain, what enlightenment *is*.

You know those old black-and-white TV shows where the crazy, out-of-control computer is causing mayhem, and the hero destroys the machine by forcing it to ponder something imponderable? The unit's reel-to-reels spin helplessly as it repeats, *"Does-not-compute..."* And finally its demise is signaled when steam rises out of its casing.

It's kind of like that. We, the crazy CPUs, would be steaming all over the place. It wouldn't destroy our circuits, of course (that only happens on TV). But the enlightened state would be utterly imponderable nonetheless, because an ego mind can't hope to grasp the very thing its existence is meant to hide.

If it's the ego mind that keeps us from being able to define and describe what enlightenment is, then one would assume an enlightened person would have no trouble at all with it. And yet I suspect it's almost as difficult for them to answer the question, *what is enlightenment?* as it is for the rest of us. Partly because the enlightened state does not contain anything in it that can actually be described—and partly because, as I mentioned earlier, human language is all but useless for such tasks.

Do you find you're still hanging onto some fixed ideas about enlightenment, despite the fact that we've shown it's impossible for you to know what this state is actually like? I'm not surprised. Most of us who harbor a desire for awakening hold preconceived ideas of what enlightenment must be like—I know I did—but the truth is, you really have no clue and neither do I. And everyone who is not permanently awakened is in this same boat.

Do I honestly know through firsthand experience what enlightenment is? No. This is the kind of uncompromising self-examination that helps us let go of the need to be right, as we realize we really don't know what we thought we knew.

Realizing you don't know is, if not half the battle, at least the first meaningful step toward the end of the war.

• • •

Adyashanti is a permanently awakened guy. I like his forthright style of explanation as he describes, to the best of his ability, his own state of awareness. This is one of the ways Adya describes the nature of enlightenment: He says it isn't about becoming something; he says it's about *unbecoming what isn't.*

And that makes sense to me. The ego mind is a false construct that's layered overtop of the natural self. To reject the ego's influence would be to reveal the true self that's no longer blocked by egoic perception. What that true self actually is—this is what I have no clue about.

I've often thought perceiving with the ego mind seems very much like being under the influence of a powerful narcotic. Adya seems to agree; he has at times referred to egoic perception as the ultimate altered state of consciousness.

Enlightenment, then, must mean kicking the habit. Getting that ego drug out of your system. So I guess you might say enlightenment is the state in which you're no longer high.

Does that clear things up any?

You're welcome.

ENLIGHTENMENT VERSUS AWAKENING

The ego mind is a fictional "me" self completely focused on getting its own way. Everything it does is designed to protect itself and get its needs met, so it can become happy. Of course, that never actually happens. The ego can never be completely happy or satisfied just as it is; as we talked about earlier, there's always something preventing total contentment.

This fictional "me" self is nothing but a deeply ingrained pattern of habitual thought and perception, built on past experiences. This ego mind is not who you really are.

The ego mind is addicted to the idea of separation. *I want what I want, so I can become happy. I don't really care whether you get what you want; your happiness is not my problem.* Because the ego is able to focus only on its own needs, it keeps the thought of separation alive, forever seeking ways to make itself stronger at the expense of others.

Wait a minute, you may be thinking, *that doesn't sound like me. My mind isn't only focused on my own wants. I care about others; I want my family and friends to be happy too. Doesn't that disprove what you're saying about my ego mind?*

Well, no. Not really. It just means you've included the welfare of those people on your list of things you need in order to be happy. Maybe your list also includes political or humanitarian causes. Or maybe your happiness depends on saving the rainforests. Whatever your personal definition of happiness and fulfillment may be, your ego mind will perpetually strive to get what it wants—knowing full well that in doing so, others with opposing priorities will be deprived of what *they* want. That's how ego minds work.

Spiritual awakening is an invitation to be free from this form of thinking. A reasonable description of what takes place during an awakening is that you suddenly realize the small, grubby, thinking mind you always assumed was "you" isn't really who you are. In the awakened state, you directly experience yourself as you are in truth: Incomparably bigger, deeper, greater than you ever imagined. One hundred percent without wants or needs. United with everything, and peaceful to your very core.

Of course, there's a catch. In an awakening, you're only seeing a glimpse of the world as it really is. If you like what you see and want to embrace this truth permanently, it means voluntarily letting go of all your old limiting beliefs about yourself and the world. Chucking all the ideas of "us versus them," on which your perception is based.

An awakening offers a real-time opportunity to choose between eternal truth and the world of illusion you currently call home.

•   •   •

Talk about being put on the spot; there you are, being offered an invitation to commune directly with all that is. But you can't very well awaken to what *is*, if you still find value in embracing what *isn't*.

So the whole experience is freaking you out a little, and you find you're just not ready to turn your back on everything you thought you knew. That's ok, no pressure. But it means this awakening, no matter how powerful, will be a mere blip on your radar screen, nothing more. A powerful blip, to be sure—but immediately after it's over, your ego mind will resume control of your existence. Just like you asked it to do.

If, on the other hand, you manage to choose truth in that moment, you will remain awake to the reality of existence. (At least partially, depending on how much truth you're able to accept at the time.) Choosing any amount of truth is not easy to do. Choosing truth means you're letting go of everything you ever believed, including everything you thought you were. Think about that for a moment: Surrendering what you think you are feels like death. Like voluntary spiritual suicide. No wonder so few of us manage to choose truth over illusion, when the opportunity arises.

Choosing truth over illusion is what this book is for. An everyday practice of Oneness helps strengthen our sanity. Maybe this additional strength and sanity will help prepare us, if we happen to find ourselves being offered that sudden invitation to choose the truth of all existence.

Toward that end, this book contains lots of practical exercises designed (by Spirit) to help us see the world more clearly. As daily life presents its false dramas to us, we can train ourselves not to be taken in by the ego's interpretation of events, instead looking deep within to ask: *What am I really? And what is the world?*

Over time this kind of daily practice strengthens our ability to tell truth from illusion. And as we align ourselves more and more with truth, the surrender of what's false gets easier.

CHAPTER THREE

hysterical blindness

BITS AND PIECES

In the prodigal child story, we explored the reasons we're so reluctant to return to the memory of Oneness.

Yet some of us eventually override that fear, as we consciously develop an authentic desire to wake up and remember our true nature. And that's when we discover this waking up business can be a little easier said than done.

I was recently asked this question:

I've finally decided I want ultimate truth. It seems to me this decision alone ought to be enough to make it happen. I've made the conscious choice for sanity and peace—why is it still so damn hard to release the ego?

And this was my answer:

Any of us can awaken permanently to the truth, just by wanting the truth wholeheartedly, with all parts of the mind united and sure of what it wants. Yet one of the hallmarks of an ego mind is that it doesn't see anything in a single-minded way. So even though a small part of my conscious mind has firmly committed to Oneness, all the other parts of my fragmented mind are not so firmly committed to the truth of Oneness. Some of them are pretty firmly committed to the opposite.

It's kind of like the truth of Oneness is a rosebud in my hand; I can feel it, I can smell it, I know it's there... yet I can't help but see it through a fragmented, kaleidoscopic lens. A hundred partial images adding up to nothing that looks anything like a rosebud. So I'm left with only that one small part of my mind that wants the fragrant, rosy truth.

Our ever-shifting kaleidoscopic perception is the reason our spiritual paths never seem to forge a straight line from Point A to Point B. We think (and hope) we're heading directly toward awakening, but the truth is, as we leave Point A behind and set off boldly for parts unknown, you and I wouldn't recognize Point B if it bit us in the ass.

• • •

Point B is eternal truth—and eternal truth is upside down from our current belief system. That's why sometimes a practice of Oneness feels like the loss of everything we hold dear. Corrected perception, if we were to manage it all at once, would metaphorically send our chandeliers crashing to the floor, while scattering our furniture all over the ceiling.

Think of the mess.

To our ego mind, that seems like the worst sort of chaos. The ego will do its utmost to help us avoid corrected perception at all costs.

So how did we get ourselves into this predicament, and what are we up against in trying to undo the process? I can share with you some detailed visions Spirit has shown me on this subject. These symbolic explanations have helped me understand the challenges involved in healing my own split perception; you may find them useful as well.

For example, I've been shown the workings of my own ego mind, and the torturous things it does to keep the illusion of separation in place. The lesson I'm about to share with you took place in an hours-long revelatory vision I will describe for you as best I can, using the same visual symbols I was shown at the time:

Picture an infinitely large, clear pane of glass, floating in a vast universe. That's a visual metaphor for all of us, together in Oneness; the truth can clearly be seen as it flows unimpeded through us.

We decide to pretend we've cracked into separate bits. It isn't possible in truth, so we resort to self-trickery to make it seem as if it's so: We pretend to etch a multitude of cracks on the surface of the glass, and then, through intense concentration and belief, we imagine these cracks to be real.

Once this feat of illusion is accomplished, we break the cracks into small individual shards, by focusing our minds on the creation of imaginary gaps between the cracks. These gaps are held in place by firm belief; the belief seems to be made of a clenched sort of energy field. This energy field makes the gaps appear "solid," which obscures any connection between shards.

(I should take a moment to explain that although I was standing to the side as an observer of all this, I was at the same time also gently experiencing everything I was being shown. So I could feel the powerful energy field between those fake gaps, and recognized how profoundly exhausting it was to keep that permanent energy spasm going.)

With the formation of these small shards and fake gaps, we've achieved a basic illusion of separation—yet that's only the first step of the process. It's individuality that we're really after. To achieve this, the shards voluntarily twist just a bit, each one pointed in a slightly different direction from all the others. This guarantees that nothing can be viewed exactly the same way by any two shards, because each is seeing from a unique perspective.

(As I watched the shards twist, I dimly felt the constant pain each shard willingly endures by choosing to remain out of alignment with truth.)

The ego has invested quite a lot of ingenuity and effort in

helping us live out our fantasy of individuality. Its survival depends on our willingness to sustain this illusion; it has no intention of making it easy for us to change our minds and return to Oneness instead. To safeguard its investment, it works to cover its tracks, making sure no shard can ever again perceive anything as it really is. To do this, our perception must be scrambled:

Each of us carries within our twisted shard a distorted prism of perception based on past hurts, disappointments, yearnings or triumphs. Every experience each of us collects here in the 3-D dream world is catalogued carefully by the ego, with past outcomes forming our expectation of how the world will behave in the future. No two prisms are alike.

Everything we see is filtered and bent through this prism of past memory projected onto the present. We find it virtually impossible to see any circumstance just as it is; we have no choice but to view it in light of what our individual prisms show us about our expectations of the world.

Yet this is not enough distortion to keep the ego's thought system safe from the truth. Another tool is needed to guarantee we'll never return to the root of the problem and restore our unified vision.

(Do you remember those trick viewing scopes they used to sell in the backs of comic books? The ones you could use to see around corners and spy on your friends? That's what I was shown next.)

Each individual prismatic shard is equipped with its own spy scope. So now, when any individual shard looks straight ahead, it's really seeing something that's happening around a hidden corner, perceived through a series of angled mirrors.

So anything we try to do or change or fix within this illusory dream of separateness is doomed to fail, because we're perceiving the problem as being right in front of us, when in fact it's someplace else entirely. Each of us is flailing around blindly, responding to things that aren't really there, yet believing the images directly in front of us are absolutely real.

And as I stood outside and also inside this symbolic vision with Spirit, I realized how painful it is to keep up this elaborate hoax of separateness. And that's my real point in telling you this story. I could both see and feel how sick, sad and confused my egoic perception actually was; how far removed it was from anything resembling truth. And I understood that every sliver of the "split" mind is in the same predicament and yearns to return to sanity, whether it consciously realizes it or not.

Yet that split is held in place on the deepest unconscious levels of the mind, so it's damn near impossible to get in there and heal the whole thing on our own. In my experience, a higher power is needed for that.

Many spiritual devotees are quite comfortable with the notion of a higher power. Many are not. If this quasi-religious description creeps you out, call it anything you like; we're really just talking about your own highest self. The you that isn't fooled by the fantasy of separation. The you that already knows it's One with all that is.

Not everybody agrees about the necessity of that higher power partnership, of course. This is just my observation based on my own experience. The decision whether or not to call upon divine help seems to depend entirely on the spiritual background of the person in question.

Most of the enlightened guys I've read have come from a Zen tradition (in which one would tend not to pair up with a higher power), or from Hinduism (in which one might), or even from no spiritual tradition at all. Jed McKenna, for instance, says his own path to enlightenment was not spiritual; he was merely hell bent on realizing the truth. He says there's nothing of Spirit in his awakening, and describes his enlightenment as something akin to total emptiness.

I've looked carefully within to see if total emptiness resonates with me, and it doesn't. My relationship with Spirit is too deep for that. Too alive, too much an inextricable part of myself—and merging more indelibly with my essential self all the time. I had to conclude, therefore, after months of determined self-inquiry, that the friendship and guidance of a higher self feels true for me all the way down to the core of my being. So at least for now, I'm forced to jettison the firsthand experience of several enlightened people in favor of my own.

Not like I've made an exhaustive research project of studying every book by every enlightened person. I haven't. I pick up only the ones I feel called to read, and leave the rest. But of all the ones I've felt compelled to read, only a couple of them speak of having a direct relationship with a Heavenly presence of unconditional love. None speak of having been shown limitless patience and perfect gentleness by a Heavenly guide or teacher while they underwent their dismantling process. So none of their experiences seem to line up exactly with mine.

Does that mean I'm not actually on the track to enlightenment? Maybe. Or maybe there are lots and lots of tracks, and each one gets dismantled in its own unique way. It was hard at first, being unable to point to anyone else's similar experience as reassurance that mine is correct. But I'm at peace now with the seeming singularity of my own path.

It wasn't an easy decision initially to reject the firsthand experience of those who are permanently awake, just because their experiences seem to differ from mine. Yet all any of us really has to go on is our own authentic experience. We shouldn't even take the unquestioned word of a person who is urging us not to take anyone's unquestioned word for it. We've got to be self-reliant and decide all things for ourselves.

The road to enlightenment is an entirely personal journey. Others may appear on the path from time to time to point us in the right direction, but every step we take is our own.

• • •

The decision to choose my own direct experience over that of the enlightened folks was partly the result of self-inquiry, but also it was an after-effect of the first big awakening in 2005. That experience left a sort of residue of truth behind. A lasting connection to the big picture, if you will, coupled with a strong sense that I had no choice but to follow my own path from then on, and nobody else's.

Personality-wise, I'm not so big on wandering the untrammeled wilderness all by myself, machete in hand, bushwhacking a brand-new path as I go. I tend to prefer the road more traveled. Once I find a trustworthy vehicle (first Buddhism, then *A Course in Miracles*), I want to get on the bus and let somebody else drive the well-worn path for me.

But no. I seem to be a solo explorer, whether I like it or not. Having seen a bit of the true nature of reality during that first awakening, I became unable to follow any previously established spiritual path. It had nothing to do with the validity of the path in question; it was all about teaching me to trust my own firsthand experiences and make my own choices. So I left my beloved Buddhist practice behind, and began learning how to follow my own path and nobody else's. Years later, I find I'm still following my own path and nobody else's.

That first awakening kicked my butt in so many ways. Yet powerful as it was, it still showed me only a glimpse of the truth. And let's face it: A glimpse, no matter how life-changing, is not the same thing as living the full enlightened truth.

Don't get me wrong, a glimpse of the truth is a wonderful thing. But it should never be trusted unquestioningly, by me or you or anybody. A glimpse of the truth is like that parable about the blind guy describing an elephant: He reports with absolute firsthand authority that an elephant is shaped like a snake, long and thin and curvy. He's not wrong. The part of the elephant he touched was exactly like that. But after hearing his report, how much closer are we to knowing anything at all about elephants?

Consequently, each time I move forward into uncharted territory I never automatically assume I've found the right way. I still look to the enlightened guys periodically to see which way their fingers are pointing. And then I question deeply, because I recognize that all responsibility for the direction I choose to go next is entirely up to me.

THE DINNER TABLE AWAKENING

So now I want to talk a little bit about what actually took place in that first awakening, the one I refer to as "The Dinner Table Awakening of 2005." At various times I've described it in different ways, using different metaphors to explain it from various angles. None of those descriptions really matter, because there are no words for what actually took place; like I said, direct spiritual experience is just plain beyond anything words can describe. Yet this time, I'm not interested in symbolically describing it. I want to break it down for you, tell you what my responses were, sort of as a play-by-play.

In this awakening, I was presented with an invitation to accept enlightenment. (As I said earlier, that's what awakenings are—you're awakened, at least partially, to the truth of all existence. But whether you take that opportunity to embrace the truth or turn away from it is up to you.)

The truth presented itself and then waited serenely for my response.

And I didn't embrace it. At the time I found the limitless freedom of enlightenment so disturbing, so profoundly uncomfortable, that I willingly threw away the opportunity. Although I realized I really *ought* to want the truth of all existence, at the time there was way too much darkness in me, to be able to stand all that light.

That light, by the way, is infinitely gentle and non-judging. Completely impartial. You might even go so far as to call it sublimely indifferent; the light merely is. There's nothing in the light itself that ever could, or would, cause pain. It was my reaction to the light that was the problem. I wasn't worthy; I couldn't stand to be seen. And I desperately wanted boundaries and limitations and corners in which to hide. Yet there were none.

I did try to accept this limitless freedom and radiant purity for what seemed an eon, yet was probably more like ten or fifteen seconds—but there was no getting used to it. My need for a hiding place was too strong. So I voluntarily pulled myself back into my body and my 3-D world instead, choosing to reject Oneness.

Could I kick myself now for having made that choice? For not trying a little harder while I had the chance? Uh...*yes*. My ego mind could wallow in self-criticism over that one if I let it. But clearly I wasn't ready to embrace the truth; no matter how high the stakes, I just couldn't stand to stay one moment longer in that infinite state of awareness.

• • •

Over the years, I've had dozens of conversations with Spirit about the truth of all existence. Or, to be more accurate: I've had conversations with a loving, patient presence that I have concluded must be of divine origin. I choose to call it Spirit, but I'm pretty sure it would answer to just about any name I might want to give it. Yet after rigorous self-inquiry, I must admit I can't be one hundred percent certain who or what that presence actually is.

I once asked it, "Hey, what are you really?" And its somewhat indirect reply was, *I am the memory of God in you.* So that answer would seem to lend credence to the "it's your own highest self" description. The un-split, un-crazy self that remembers

Oneness and isn't fooled by the ego's version of the world. Or that's how I've chosen to interpret the answer, anyway. You're free to draw your own conclusions.

Anyway, although Spirit has taught me a great many things in our conversations, it's not like I can ask any old question and expect an easy answer.

Case in point: I was thoroughly disturbed by a number of things I'd read in Jed McKenna's first book,* especially his emphatic assertion that if you want to awaken permanently, it's necessary to destroy your own ego in a violent, bloody battle to the finish.

I pondered this and prayed about it, but couldn't seem to reconcile it with my own experience. Eventually I asked Spirit the question, "Hey, what's the deal with killing the ego in order to enlighten? Is Jed McKenna right? He says there's no other option. Is his take-no-prisoners description the way it really is for everybody, or is that just the way he happened to experience his own awakening?"

I got this seemingly oblique non-answer: *Jed McKenna is neither right nor wrong.*

And I had to smile, because although that answer may sound as if it were intentionally meant to frustrate my ego mind, I knew better.

In fact, the more I thought about it, the more I sensed this statement was actually a full and complete answer containing fathomless worlds of depth within it. I didn't yet understand it, but I had the feeling I would, someday soon.

And I realized this was one of Spirit's classic "time-release" teachings: A carefully measured dose of wisdom perfectly designed to cure what ails me—just not until a little later on when I'm more ready to swallow it, and digest this particular bit of medicine.

*Spiritual Enlightenment: The Damndest Thing. It's part one of his enlightenment trilogy.

THE EGO AS ENEMY - PART I

This is what I don't get about the "murder your own ego" method of waking up: All conflict is manufactured by the ego. So it would seem that making an enemy of the ego mind plays right into the trap it has set for you; getting into a battle with your own ego mind, in other words, is just going to nourish and strengthen your ego mind.

To prepare your mind for awakening is to dismantle the ego's thought system, thereby gradually weakening it as you simultaneously starve it of fuel. Yet if you subscribe to the epic battle method of ego removal, it seems to me that every day you'd be offering your ego mind a big, juicy struggle sandwich.

That strikes me as remarkably inefficient. Of course, it's mighty hard not to hold some kind of grudge against your own ego mind—chances are, profound disgust with the fantasy 3-D universe (and with the ego mind that holds it in place) is probably one of the primary motivating factors that's brought you this far on your quest for truth. It certainly is one of mine. This attitude shouldn't be encouraged, however—although there's no point in beating yourself up about it, either. If you find you're harboring a great, big grudge against your ego, just be aware of that motivation, and try to keep in mind nothing about the way you view the ego or the 3-D world is accurate. You're not perceiving things as they really are.

Even though ego hatred is probably unavoidable to some degree, the amount and intensity of the hatred is definitely something to keep an eye on. Try to remember ego hatred is only an expedient tool to help keep you going right now; like other paradoxes on the road to enlightenment, two opposing things about ego hatred seem to be simultaneously true and false: It isn't productive to hate your own ego, except while it sort of still is.

Yet, paradoxes aside, too much of a grudge will only slow you down. To judge and find the ego guilty just strengthens the building blocks of separation. Besides, although you might find it tempting to ego-bash, it's neither useful nor particularly fair to build up a major case against the big, bad ego mind.

After all, you yourself created the ego mind, and it serves entirely at your pleasure. If you didn't want it or need it on some level—if you had no desire at all to hide in darkness, safe from the brilliant light that is the truth of all reality—your ego mind would already be history.

CAN ENLIGHTENMENT RUB OFF?

If I hang around an enlightened person long enough, in other words, can I hope to catch enlightenment like a case of Heavenly cooties?

Short answer: Probably not. Not as far as I can tell, anyway.

I wrote the following diary entry shortly after leaving my Buddhist practice behind (and a couple of months after the Dinner Table Awakening). Originally meant for inclusion in *Long Time No See*, this entry ended up on the cutting room floor before eventually resurfacing as part of a 2010 blog post.

It's not so much the diary entry itself, but a blog comment it received that got me pondering this subject.

July 23, 2005

It still feels a little like freefall. Or no—not freefall, exactly. More like I leapt off a cliff without my Buddhist practice to protect me, and am now floating gently suspended in midair. Destination unknown.

Although I have no idea where I'm headed, I do know this: It's time for me to chart my own course. I can no longer follow the teachings of an enlightened human being.

Any enlightened human being.

Nothing against the teachers or their teachings—but ever since that brief taste of direct spiritual communion, I can't escape the feeling that human words are just a collection of inadequate symbols, incapable of expressing the living truth of spiritual experience. Even the most gifted communicator, the most eloquent and enlightened teacher, can function only as a finger pointing at the truth; it's impossible for them to transmit the truth itself.

I'm sure they would if they could. An enlightened teacher surely must know the perfect, glorious truth in all its fullness, yet would have no direct way of passing that knowledge on to others.

Because spiritual truth can only be experienced firsthand.

This was the comment I received:

You say "An enlightened teacher…would have no direct way of passing that knowledge on to others. Because spiritual truth can only be experienced firsthand."

What makes you think this, Carrie? How can you be sure a lit candle cannot light another candle?

And this was my response:

In my experience, the gap between direct spiritual communion and all worldly forms of communication is so great it's truly unbridgeable. Perhaps there are historical examples where it appeared that a lit candle lit another candle—and who am I to say it didn't happen that way?

Yet I suspect the actual causality of such an event would not be quite so direct. If a mind is truly ready, any old random thing can cause it to remember the truth.

Perhaps a student, perfectly poised to remember the truth, sought out a master whose single word sparked that memory of Heaven. And so it would appear to an onlooker that the master caused the disciple's enlightenment. Yet in reality the truth came from within—the nature of the spark was inconsequential.

That's my theory, anyway. But really, your guess is as good as mine.

• • •

Some of us don't dash around the world looking for gurus to cozy up to, yet we're susceptible to a related (if subtler) form of the same thinking. We keep an ear to the ground, perpetually in search of that special process or teaching we hope will bring about our enlightenment. We hear anecdotal evidence that somebody has awakened by using a particular method, so we leap on the bandwagon in case the same method will magically work for us too. I've certainly done this—and fairly recently, too—even though I know better.

A few months ago, I heard of a guy who permanently awakened by using the simplest method imaginable. First, he focused his intention on a strong desire for ultimate truth. Then he cleared his mind and meditated. The result was an explosive awakening; and when he was offered the invitation to release all attachment to egoic perception, he accepted it. And just like that—bang! Enlightenment.

I was deeply impressed, and decided to try it for myself. For the next two nights, I did my best to focus my mind on a clear desire for enlightenment (with less than stellar results), and then meditated. They were nice meditations, but hardly explosive.

A couple of days later I heard about a woman who self-realized after using Byron Katie's process of inquiry. She'd locked herself in her bedroom, vowing not to come out until successfully freeing herself from illusion. For about a tenth of a second, I, too, contemplated locking myself in my bedroom with a stack of Katie's work sheets. (And maybe some pretzels. In case I got hungry.)

But then I realized what these two anecdotal stories had in common: In both cases, the seeker possessed the clear determination and the readiness to awaken to the truth *right now.* The method or the place scarcely mattered.

And I already knew this, of course. When Siddhartha sat down to meditate beneath the Bodhi tree, after all, he attained his enlightenment not because there was anything extraordinary about that tree, but because he was absolutely determined to wake up—and had no intention of budging from that spot until he had done so.*

It's not like Heaven is withholding our enlightenment until we're good enough, or worthy enough to deserve it. Quite the contrary. Our One self knows we're already limitlessly perfect, just as we are right now. The trouble is, *we* don't know it. And as long as we cling to limits and imperfection, the sudden introduction of their Heavenly opposite is likely to blow our minds. And not in a good way. Our One self knows this, and spares us that pain.

Look around you: Everything you see, everybody you encounter is the potential spark for enlightenment. The truth is everywhere, just waiting for you to stop arguing with it. To stop denying it and resisting it and blocking it out of your memory.

As far as I can tell, the readiness and willingness to surrender our belief in imperfection is the one and only prerequisite for enlightenment. And that readiness comes from retraining our minds to overlook the ego's stories, and put our trust in ultimate truth instead.

So, back to that original question about playing with fire: Yes, a lit candle can surely light another candle—but only if the

---

*Spoiler alert: After attaining enlightenment, Siddhartha became known as Buddha, and... well, you know the rest.

second wick is thoroughly prepared to receive the flame.

Like I said earlier, one or two people per generation might spontaneously awaken fully, without any conscious effort. I guess their wicks are just naturally ready, and that's wonderful for them. But I'm fairly sure the rest of us have work to do.

EXPEDIENT MEANS

If you get far enough down the road to Oneness, eventually you realize through direct, firsthand experience that nothing in this 3-D universe is true or real. It becomes obvious the dismantling of your world will require you to let go of everything you ever believed in—everything that ever played a role in the formation of your personality-self and your worldview.

Most of us humans need help embracing this path to Oneness, which is completely counterintuitive and unlike anything we've ever known. To take away all belief systems before somebody is ready to release them voluntarily would not be a particularly kind or helpful thing to do. That would just freak a person out needlessly.

This is where expedient means teachings come in. "Expedient means" is a Buddhist term that refers to teachings that are partly or mostly false and misleading, yet are designed to reach learners at whatever level of understanding they currently possess. And once they've expanded their worldviews to include this teaching, it's gently (or sometimes not so gently) taken away, and replaced with a more sophisticated teaching that's a bit closer to the truth than the one before it. And so it goes.

In my experience, Spirit makes masterful use of expedient means teachings. None of us starts out able to accept the full truth. It's through expedient means teachings that we are gradually taught to discern for ourselves the false from the true. And once we discern it, we can choose correctly between them.

There's no limit to what constitutes an expedient means teaching. It isn't just spiritual philosophies or religious teachings that qualify. If we're willing, Spirit can turn any everyday occurrence into an expedient means teaching opportunity. No matter what issues or obstacles we think we face, no matter what temptations or distractions appear in our lives, Spirit can take any shiny object we're fascinated with, and turn it into a perfect and beautiful expedient means lesson of lasting value.

And that takes the heat off us completely. If we make a mistake along the road, in Spirit's loving hands the error is dusted off and shown to us in a light that causes us to understand a bit more of the truth. How fortunate, then, to have made the mistake in the first place! Or if we're tempted to dabble in a teaching that seemingly conflicts with our own current belief system, Spirit gently shows us the conflict exists only in our ego imagination; after all, in ultimate truth no conflict is possible.

As I've said before, nobody's path is a straight line between points A and B. Every sideways step or seemingly false move has its own beautiful purpose. It took me a long time to realize this. My tendency when presented with a teaching of great power and truth was to latch onto that single teaching, and rigidly refuse to pay attention to any other forms of help that appeared on my path, for fear the purity of my chosen belief system would become diluted.

That's perfectly ok; it's one way of doing it. Yet such a fundamentalist approach really isn't necessary. I understand now if we hold a constant desire for truth in our hearts, Spirit is free to use absolutely everything in our lives as fuel for teaching us the truth of Oneness.

CHAPTER FOUR

the serious beginning

QUESTION EVERYTHING

The decision to question everything is the heart of the quest for enlightenment; it's the fire that turns your unfocused wish for self-realization into a serious beginning. In fact, those few words are so important, let's back up and give them their own set of capital letters: The Serious Beginning. The Serious Beginning is the refusal to take any part of your world at face value. It's the willingness to sincerely question anything and everything about your life as you know it. To burn your own house down if necessary, because that's how badly you want the truth.

Do I really know what I think I know?

Or do I just want to believe I know the truth?

What do I know for certain?

These are the questions you will learn to ask yourself about everything in your world.

• • •

Let me save you some time: There's virtually nothing you know for certain, because everything you "know" and everything you think or imagine or believe is a product of your ego mind.

You know you exist in some way, and that's about it. And frankly, even that knowledge is pretty iffy when it comes right down to it. And everything else is just a bunch of stories.

So your spiritual practice becomes one of self-inquiry to determine for yourself what's true—and then to let go of what's false. But of course, you shouldn't take my word for it. Everything you read in books must be questioned too, and then released.

This letting-go process needn't always be painful or frightening, by the way. Yes, the quest for enlightenment brings with it anarchy in the truest sense; it is the systematic overthrow of everything you believe in. But whether that's a bloody revolution or a relatively peaceful transition of power is up to you.

A dear friend demonstrated the concept this way recently as we walked together on a beach: He bent down and picked up a small, smooth pebble, enclosing it in his fist. "There are two ways of letting go," he said, "but only one of them involves loss." Holding his fist out toward me with the palm facing down, he opened his fingers and the pebble dropped to the ground.

Kneeling to pick up the same stone, he once again enclosed it in his fist. This time he turned his hand palm side up. As he opened his fingers, the pebble stayed comfortably where it was, yet without attachment.

A nice way of looking at what could otherwise be perceived as a pretty bleak or terrifying process, don't you think? Armed with this relatively gentle model for letting go, self-inquiry doesn't seem nearly so daunting.

At least to me. At least so far.

You may feel differently about it, of course.

•   •   •

If you're serious about beginning, you'll question everything deeply—even your spiritual beliefs. Especially your spiritual beliefs.

If they're perfectly aligned with truth, let them go. They'll remain in your hand, at least for a while, as you walk your path to awakening. If they're less than perfectly aligned with truth, let them go and they'll begin to dissolve like all the other parts of your illusory dream state.

This process of awakening is destructive; it is the dismantling of everything you ever thought was true. But in my experience it needn't necessarily be cruel or violent, unless you happen to like it that way. And as far as I can tell, it doesn't always have to involve loss. You do, however, need to proceed with the assumption that all things *may* be lost. After all, your palm is open now. Some things might unexpectedly jump out of their own accord. If they do, let them go.

The Serious Beginning is an insatiable hunger for the truth of existence. An unflagging desire to bring an end to all dreams.

Even the really nice ones.

Even the really ugly ones.

It means you have to be willing, even eager, to dig up every bit of darkness, denial and unconscious fantasy you find in yourself, face it squarely and examine what it's made of. *Is it true?* No, sweetie, it's not true. Like every other product of your ego mind, it's a lie. So your job is to release it. No exceptions.

This is the Serious Beginning. This is the road to enlightenment. I'm pretty sure there is no other.

TRUST, FAITH AND BELIEF – PART I

Trust, faith and belief are wonderful companions. Together, they'll get you a good, long way down the road to self-realization. All three of these tools are temporary; none of them will be needed after split perception is replaced by Oneness. However, of the three, belief must be jettisoned long before the other two.

For the serious seeker—and by that I mean a person who wants the truth of all reality, come hell or high water—belief is abandoned sooner rather than later. That's because all belief is of the ego, and the longer you stay stuck in a belief system, the more you'll spin your wheels and get nowhere nearer your goal.

It doesn't matter how fine or correct the belief; that's not the point. To firmly believe in one thing is to firmly disbelieve in something else. The ego mind keeps a tight grip on what it agrees with, while rejecting what it dislikes. As a result, rigid barriers remain intact between the two.

In the truth of Oneness, barriers of any kind could never exist; this exclusionary form of thinking is only made possible by the illusion of duality and separation, courtesy of your ego mind.

•   •   •

Fear is the engine that powers our 3-D world of illusion; judgment is its fuel. And belief is the glue that holds the entire fantasy of separation together. These are the raw materials your ego mind uses to keep the world in place.

The role of belief in this process should not be underestimated. There's a reason they call it make-believe, after all. Belief is the stuff fantasy is made of. Discarding belief is a step all serious students must learn to take.

Discarding belief is not the same thing as disbelief, by the way. Disbelief is equally of the ego, being merely the flipside of belief. Let me show you what I mean: If I pull on Santa's beard, for example, and in so doing discover that's really my next-door neighbor in the red velvet suit, my belief in Santa Claus will suffer irreparable damage. *I know for a fact this guy does not live at the North Pole*, I think to myself. *And he doesn't make toys for a living—he works at the brewery across town.* So although I used to wholeheartedly believe in Santa, having been shown damning evidence that an impostor is at work, I reject my previous belief. I judge my previous belief to have been erroneous, and now I disbelieve in Santa.

To truly lay aside belief, on the other hand, is to practice non-judgment. It means looking at this 3-D world and seeing it as it is, refusing to assign it any meaning it doesn't inherently possess.

Let's use the guy in the Santa suit again as an example. *My neighbor in a red velvet suit.* That's what you'd think, because really, that's all you're seeing. Of course you'd still recognize it as a Santa suit; to practice non-judgment is not the same thing as getting a lobotomy. But the recognition would bring no automatic acceptance or rejection with it. There's nothing here to believe or disbelieve, no stories to tell yourself about it. The guy in the Santa suit merely *is*.

This process of non-judgment starves your ego mind of its customary fuel. The refusal to believe or disbelieve sends the ego to bed without supper.

•   •   •

"Ok, Carrie," I hear you say, "point taken about belief and disbelief. But you say belief should go, yet faith can stay. Faith and belief seem so similar. Isn't it splitting hairs to distinguish between them?"

Well, maybe. I would explain the difference this way:

Let's say you're at a point in your quest for enlightenment where you're ready to voluntarily let go of all the beliefs that have gotten you through life thus far. You've asked to take this next step into the unknown, and as with the many steps that have come before it, you find you still need trust and faith to see you through.

Because it's still scary, the big unknown. Even though you yourself asked for it. Now more than ever, you'll want to summon the trust that this action of stepping forward blindly without stories is the right thing to do. And the faith that you'll find something solid to step on when you get there.

You no longer hold fixed beliefs about who or what might be helping or supporting you along the way. That's a bit scary. But you've decided to go for it anyway, based on previous outcomes. Call it a calculated risk.

The decision to let go of belief means a new commitment to enlightenment has been made. You have stated plainly to the universe that you prefer truth to fantasy, and you don't care if that preference has a seeming price.

You squarely face the fear that it's entirely possible your trust and faith are misplaced—after all, you can't be absolutely sure anything will be there to support you after you leap. You're questioning everything, now. Are you certain your trust and faith will be rewarded in the future, just because they seemed to bring you support in the past? No. But you offer your trust and faith anyway; you're willing to be proven wrong in making that choice.

So after belief is set aside, it seems we still have use for trust and faith (at least for a while). But now we agree to take that next step, while at the same time accepting the possibility our faith may go unrewarded—that there may be nothing at all waiting there to support us.

Since we have no real firsthand access to truth as long as we're caught up in this delusional belief system of separation, we need to hang onto faith and trust throughout the process. Faith that truth is waiting to be revealed after the false sense of self is gone, and trust that it's worth sticking with this quest as all familiar signposts and safe harbors vanish along the way.

Your ego mind will be quick to point out if nothing is there to support you after you leap, that means you're headed for the void of non-existence. The void of non-existence is the ego's deepest fear; it wants this to be your deepest fear, too.

We reach a point where the desire for enlightenment (to be rid of the false personality-self and embrace truth instead) is stronger than the need to hide behind that false self. This is when we begin to side against the ego by letting go of belief. As our beliefs crumble, so crumbles the false self.

And in undertaking this demolition project, we accept that it means we'll be heading into the scary void of no-self, to discover who we really are without the individual "me."

Maybe the void is real, and maybe it's only another lie told by the ego. We won't know until we turn to face it squarely and see what it's made of. Either way, it doesn't stop us. And that means the ego mind now has fewer and fewer bargaining chips. You've significantly reduced the ego's power, because you're not as afraid of the void as you once were.

This is when practice gets serious.

That's right, you're a Serious Beginner. You ain't afraid of no void.

You want the truth at all costs. If it turns out there actually *is* a void and you fall in, so be it. That's ok too, as long as there's truth in there.

As belief is discarded bit by bit and non-judgment is automatically strengthened, the ego's grip weakens. After all, what more is there to fear if you've already begun to accept the possibility of the void?

(EN)LIGHTEN UP!

I thought maybe we could use a little breather here; this "void of non-existence" business can seem quite grim at first glance. We'll revisit the subject more thoroughly later on; that later discussion might help allay any concerns you have about it. (Or it might not.)

Anyway, this strikes me as an excellent time to take a short break and point out yet another paradox I've noticed on my own road to enlightenment: The more serious I get about personal demolition, the more fun I have.

The more I break down the egoic stories I tell myself about me and my relationship to the world, the easier it becomes to see through those stories altogether.

What was once painful or shameful or deadly serious, now starts to look deliciously absurd. Downright goofy.

I find I laugh a lot more these days.

- *Knock knock.*
- *Who's there?*
- *Exactly.*

As the personality-self dissolves bit by bit, this just might become the funniest damn joke you've ever heard.

TRUST, FAITH AND BELIEF – PART II

Ok, back to business.

Let me give you a personal example of continuing to use trust and faith after belief has gone. The self-inquiry process I follow is to look with a very clear, unprejudiced eye at everything I think I know. Ultimately I'll have to examine each belief system on which I've built my self-identification. But for this example, let's just focus on my spiritual belief systems.

With rigorous self-honesty, I ask: *Do I know for sure this belief is true?* So far, the answer has always been no. I can't be one hundred percent sure of any of it. I wasn't there with the Israelites when the Red Sea parted; I'm taking third-hand Buddhist assurances that the Ceremony in the Air actually took place (in mid-air or otherwise), as described in the Lotus Sutra.

It gets a bit trickier when my personal, firsthand experiences enter into it. After all, I've witnessed or heard or felt a lot of powerful spiritual stuff for myself. I've repeatedly been shown truth by a loving presence of divine origin. At least I think I have. Those experiences have seemed very profound and also completely unlike anything available to me in this world.

But I have no absolute proof of who or what that all-loving, all-seeing presence actually is. Maybe it's my own ego mind, making a last-ditch effort to keep me contained within its dream web by impersonating that which I hope is waiting for me after I've awakened. I really can't say for sure.

On the other hand, these frequent communications are a very real fact of my existence. My true mind is strengthened, and my sanity steadily increases as I practice its recommendations, and listen to its gentle teachings about the meaningless unreality of this 3-D world.

I know this because I experience the benefit of ever-increasing clarity and peace. My trust in this unseen presence does not seem to be misplaced; it has never steered me off course even for a moment. I have faith it will likely continue to lead me toward my own freedom.

I acknowledge I might be completely wrong about all of that. But this course of action, this process of self-discovery, feels right. And in the absence of knowing anything for sure, I can only go by what feels right.

Belief is gone. When that loving presence communicates with me, I no longer worry about who, specifically, is doing the talking. There is talking, and that's enough for me right now.

I realize I don't know what "the memory of God in me" actually means. There's a lot of wiggle room in that statement. I used to make assumptions about its true identity, but I find I can't anymore. I haven't decided definitively that the voice *isn't* the Holy Spirit or God or an angel or a guide. I'm just saying I don't know that it is, either. I've stopped telling myself stories about it.

In the absence of stories, freedom begins.

FAITH VERSUS BLIND FAITH

As I said earlier, everything in this book is based on my own direct experiences in faith. In areas where I dig into subject matter beyond my current state of awareness (enlightenment, for example), I rely on conversations I've had with Spirit on the subject, as well as my own small glimpses into that state.

Along the way, Spirit has shared lots of interesting tools and exercises that are working well for me in my own practice of faith, so I'm including them all in the second part of this book. I've also been shown some common pitfalls of practice that I can help you watch out for.

If it interests you, I encourage you to roll up your sleeves and put this information into practice for yourself. Have your own experiences with it. Your personal experience is what authentic faith is based on.

And that's the real point I want to make here. All faith is a little bit blind; we're never able to see that next step, yet we gather our courage and make the leap anyway. But it's meant to be a calculated risk based on previous performance. For faith to be a dependable vehicle, it has to be based on personal experience. As we pray or meditate, we feel something; we see a recognizable effect. By doing that over and over, trust in the process gradually develops. It's that trust—based on experience—that makes deeper leaps of faith a good proposition: *This process has never let me down so far; I'll go a bit deeper this time and see what happens.*

Blind faith, on the other hand, is for suckers. When the going gets rough and skies are stormy, you'll discover too late that blind faith will dissolve away just when you need it most.

Why? Because you've built your house on a foundation of sugar cubes.

HOW CAN I TELL IF I'M DOING IT RIGHT?

My readership seems to be pretty evenly divided between those who, like me, have had lots of powerful spiritual experiences, and those who wish they did. The good news for that second group is, spiritual experiences actually have very little to do with Serious Beginnings, and are by no means mandatory. Still, I thought it might be useful to address this question here, because so many people do seem to be preoccupied with it.

Awhile ago, a reader asked me the question, *"How can I tell if I'm doing it right?"* At the time, her spiritual practice included a form of meditation and visualization mentioned by Gary Renard in *The Disappearance of the Universe.* It involved picturing a circle of light, and then allowing that light to expand freely. It's a beautiful meditation that's all about Oneness. Except she wasn't seeing any light. And she was therefore convinced she must have been doing it wrong.

I knew just what she meant. Back when I first started meditating, I could never get over the idea I was doing it wrong. The thought filled me with anxiety. And since I was pretty sure heightened anxiety was not what I was supposed to be feeling during meditation—well that just proved the point. I *must* have been doing it wrong. Right?

Well, no. Not really. It just took time and some very determined practice to get past the stage where my ego mind could block out all peace by shouting its messages of failure.

This is the main thing to keep in mind: Each of us is fully

equipped to realize the truth of all existence, exactly as we are right now. No extra abilities are needed. And it doesn't even matter whether we want to be equipped for it or not. Perfect Oneness is what we *are*, and we really have no say in that.

Not all of us appear to have been born with spiritual gifts. The truth is it doesn't matter. *A Course in Miracles* says if we notice an increase in our spiritual abilities as we allow our minds to be healed, it's absolutely nothing special. It's just a tiny bit of our true identity leaking in. And conversely, if we don't notice increased spiritual receptivity, that's no big deal either. The work it takes to heal our minds is the same either way.

Oh sure, it's fun to be "spiritually talented." To see visions and hear voices and dance in waves of celestial woo-woo. But it isn't necessary. And it's no reliable yardstick of spiritual advancement, either. It's just a talent, like juggling or whistling is a talent. And just like juggling or whistling, the ungifted can practice assiduously until they're reasonably skilled at it too, just like the ones who came by those gifts naturally.

So if you don't see lights when they tell you you're supposed to, no biggie. Concentrate instead on the important part: Do your best to feel the gentle expansion of freedom that is the true point of that meditation. If you can get focused enough to ignore your ego mind's critique of your meditation skills, I'm willing to bet you'll begin to feel the endless peace that comes from deep within.

And if you give it your best shot, yet still don't feel anything? Ask for help from that higher self, and then keep trying it until you do. You'll get there, I'm almost sure of it. Because no spiritual master who ever walked the Earth has anything on you. You're the complete package, the real deal. You just don't remember it yet.

IF I'M ENLIGHTENED, CAN I STILL BE WRONG?

Hell yes. Count on it, in fact.

The ego mind runs this casino you previously thought of as "the world," and like all casinos everywhere, the house always wins.

Sure, you beat the odds and won a few jackpots, and you've opened your eyes to realize how the game is played. But that doesn't mean the casino itself has actually dissolved. It just means you now know you're in a casino.

In other words, you've awakened from the dream that you're a separate mind housed in an individual body, but you're still walking around with that body. You're still negotiating your way through the deeply unconscious workings of the world. Mistakes will be made while you figure out how to manage this.

And there's more: Just because you've awakened, it doesn't mean all parts of your mind have let go of their clingy or resistant tendencies at once. It would be great if it worked that way (and maybe for a very few people it does), but from what I can tell, enlightenment seems to be an ongoing process. Your darkest unconscious crap will probably linger awhile, so the work of embracing truth and dispelling illusion will likely continue even after a permanent awakening. It seems there will be plenty left to do, as the walls of your personal casino must still come down, brick by illusory brick.

CHAPTER FIVE

down to earth

CHASING YOUR BLISS

Awakening is not about bliss or ecstasy or transcendent woo-woo experiences awash in perfect joy. That's not what the road to enlightenment is about, and apparently it's not what enlightenment itself is about, either. These beautiful states of being are sometimes a by-product of the awakening process, but seem to have nothing to do with actual awakening. This was a tough concept for me to accept, because I do enjoy the woo-woo.

The flat denial of a link between enlightenment and bliss had been stated publicly many times by self-realized teachers I respected, but still I refused to hear it. Until my Serious Beginning, that is. Until I examined my cherished notion of marshmallow-cloud enlightenment, and recognized it as fantasy. It took a good, long while, but I've finally relinquished my pursuit of spiritual practice as a means of feeling good.

Feeling good was the whole reason I was first drawn to spirituality; I became a Nichiren Buddhist because it offered me a powerful way to ease my pain and attract positive stuff into my life. There's absolutely nothing wrong with a desire to feel better, by the way. It served its purpose beautifully. I would never have become interested in spiritual practice without it.

I chased those rewards for twenty years and would have been content to do it for twenty more, but my first awakening experience in 2005 changed all that. Suddenly I wanted spiritual growth for its own sake. No more chanting for good things to happen, no more using my spiritual practice as a means to feel better.

I quit Buddhism after that awakening and began a yearlong "homework" phase, in which Spirit provided the expedient means books and teachings that would bring me up to speed on New Thought spirituality. (I was a blank slate; I knew nothing of any spiritual teaching outside Nichiren Buddhism.) And at the end of that homework year, Spirit once again wiped the slate clean and introduced yet another teaching—this one designed to carry me until I would have no further need of teachings.

It was *A Course in Miracles* (also called ACIM, for short). ACIM blew my mind, rocked my world. Yet without realizing it, I still unconsciously practiced it as a means to feel better. I was just deferring when that better feeling was supposed to arrive.

Sure, I had stopped praying for good things to happen in the short term. And I had begun to cultivate a strong desire for enlightenment as well. Except my version of that eventual enlightened state was nothing short of constant bliss. Well, maybe there would be some unconditional love and infinite peace in there too, but mostly just pure bliss. I was sure of it.

ACIM, when practiced properly, is damned difficult work. But I didn't mind the sometimes uncomfortable job of learning to forgive this illusory dream world, because I supposed there was an unimaginably beautiful enlightened state waiting for me right around the next corner. A state of awareness in which nothing ever perturbed or disturbed. Uninterrupted joy, forever and ever, amen.

Yeah, right.

We regular folks spend most of our time trying to feel better; it's what our ego minds are compelled to do. We're consumed with the pursuit of happiness and the avoidance of pain. So it should come as no surprise that even in our spiritual lives, it's easy to get stuck in the same desire to feel good. And there's absolutely nothing wrong with that. But take it from one who's been there: If pleasure-seeking is what drives you, don't expect a permanent awakening anytime soon.

Because that's really not what the authentic road to enlightenment is about. Dismantling your own cherished illusions is difficult, destructive work, and it's not always going to feel good. In fact, much of the time it likely won't feel good.

Oh sure, there will be moments of great beauty and freedom and peace; maybe even lots of them. And, God knows, the process does get lighter and more hilarious all the time. But the bulk of the work will result in discomfort. To become a Serious Beginner, you'll have to reach the point where you want the truth of all reality a whole hell of a lot more than you want to feel good.

I'm just saying.

LETTING GO

I couldn't say for sure when my Serious Beginning seriously began. I don't know precisely what triggered it, or why. I do know it started without me, and I only recognized in retrospect what had been going on.

It was 2010, and I'd been stumbling into repeated spiritual quandaries over the previous year. Although I dearly loved my practice of *A Course in Miracles*, something was gnawing insistently at my mind, urging me to look beyond all belief systems. Even that one.

I didn't want to do it. I had found a welcoming home in ACIM, and I very much wanted to stay in it. So I resisted the urge. And as we all know, resistance brings pain. After months of self-inflicted drama and confusion, this process came to a head in May of that year. I blogged about it at the time; I will repeat the gist of it here:

This is something spiritual author types hardly ever tell you: Journeys of faith are messy. Not just yours—ours, too. We merely tend to be quieter about it.

See, once you've embraced the goal of enlightenment, there really aren't any reliable signposts anymore, no matter who you are. And that can be a little, um, awkward.

Ever since my book came out (the book in which I unequivocally state that A Course in Miracles *is the last teaching I will ever need), I've been having the uncomfortable feeling I may have misstated it a bit.*

Don't get me wrong—as far as I can tell, A Course in Miracles *is a pure teaching of ultimate truth. The content is perfect. But I've been feeling like the form is not where it's at for me. And not just ACIM's form. Any teaching's form.*
It's like I keep getting prodded in the back—lovingly, gently, but very firmly—by a Heavenly billy club, while NO LOITERING signs appear all around me.

Keep moving, lady. Nothing to see here.

It all came to a head a few weeks ago. In much the same way that I was compelled to abandon my beloved Buddhist practice, this refusal to let myself stay in one spot means I have to strike out on my own all over again. To forge yet another new path through the wilderness and leave my cozy ACIM home behind.

Damn it.

So I freaked out a little. And since I don't know anything about anything, I didn't want to make any moves at all. Not only did I surrender this whole writing/speaking/ messengering gig, I actually gave it back to Spirit and walked away from it completely.

Basically, you could say it was a crisis of faith.

Except here's the funny thing: I spent a few hours drowning in the drama, but late that same night an unusual thing happened: In one of those trance-like states of neither sleeping nor waking, Spirit spent a really long time speaking to me, and I spent those same hours carefully listening.

Yet I have no idea what was said. It's not that I knew at the time but now I forget; it's more like I received the information directly into my life, bypassing my conscious mind altogether.

And when I got up the next morning, I felt no pain. No

existential angst, no drama. And since I didn't know what to do, I peacefully did nothing.

So there you have it. I'm still doing nothing. All my beliefs have once again been shaken loose and I have no idea where the hell I'm going. But thanks to Spirit, it's a very peaceful journey.

●　　　●　　　●

So now, nearly a year later, I understand what the drama was all about. It's never easy to start the dismantling process, especially if you don't yet realize that's what you're doing.

I'm also pretty sure I now understand intuitively what Spirit was telling me that night. Once the process of self-inquiry has begun, it's painful to try to hang onto unverifiable beliefs. And the more cherished the belief, the more self-inflicted trauma it causes on its way out the door. I think Spirit was alleviating the pain by teaching me to hang onto faith and trust, while letting go of belief.

The crux of my crisis was this: Both Spirit and *A Course in Miracles* say there's a state of awareness far beyond mere realization of Oneness. As we talked about earlier, a self-realized permanent awakening—according to ACIM—would only be the third stage out of a possible four.

As I have come to understand it, the third stage begins with the permanent awakening, and lasts until all unconscious pain and misperception have been healed. At that point, when perception has been completely purified, there is no more need or desire for an ego mind. And that's when the ego truly fades away forever.

After the ego mind has fully dissolved of its own accord, the fourth state of awareness is said to reveal itself. According to ACIM, this state is not something we ourselves can achieve. It's reinstated on our behalf by our One creator. Creation and creator one hundred percent reunited; a permanent homecoming, if you will.

This state, ACIM assures us, is so magnificently beyond our comprehension there's no point in even trying to describe it, other than to say it is composed of perfect, divine love.

And that's the outcome I set my sights on way back when. I wanted—and still want—that fourth stage of enlightenment. No mere permanent awakening for me. I want it all.

Yet I discovered that my belief in, and desire for, this fourth stage of enlightenment couldn't withstand self-inquiry. There was nothing in me that knew for sure this fourth stage existed.

That night, when Spirit bypassed my ego mind and spoke directly to my life, I think I was being asked to trust more. To relax my white-knuckled grip on belief, so I wouldn't remain stuck in egoic stories I had built around that fourth stage of enlightenment.

I won't lie to you; even with Spirit's intervention it wasn't what you'd call a smooth process. Until I figured out what was going on and consciously got on board with the self-inquiry process, I still endured plenty of confusion and discomfort. But eventually I did as I was asked. Using self-inquiry, I let go of my belief in that glorious future possibility of being more awakened than a permanent awakening. And with the letting go came peace.

Now that the dust has cleared somewhat, I can see my insistent belief in the fourth stage was, paradoxically, holding me back from ever being able to attain it. That's because it gave my ego mind a future fantasy to latch onto. And as long as an ego mind is fed by future fantasy, no matter what kind it is, an escape from 3-D illusion isn't likely.

Let me back up for a moment and be as clear as I can about this, because I don't want you to misunderstand my meaning:

By referring to this fourth stage of enlightenment as a future fantasy, I am in no way making a judgment about whether or not that stage exists. I'm only saying I've stopped using my belief in the fourth stage as fuel to nourish my ego mind.

The ego adores future goals, because the future never arrives. It also greatly enjoys having a rigid belief system that it can subtly embroider with its own personal stories. It's that future fantasy made of personal ego stories that I willingly released.

Anyway, I'm pretty sure letting go was the right thing to do. By releasing my grip on belief, I'm finally allowing the possibility of a fourth stage to just *be*. I've opened my palm, as it were, and that beautiful possibility of Pure Non-Dualism remains with me as I continue to walk my path.

IN THE WORLD? OR *OF* THE WORLD? – PART I

This is a place where students of Oneness get tripped up all the time. It's a lot to wrap your illusory head around; this idea that bodies aren't real and the world isn't real. Especially when you don't truly accept it yet.

Some of us do manage to authentically absorb the information that we're all One and no individual bodies are involved—but we get it on a strictly intellectual level. We then arrange our lives around that intellectual understanding.

Yet intellectual understandings are the exclusive territory of the ego. So if your personal tendency, for example, is to remove yourself from emotional complication, you'll be tempted to do the same whenever you're confronted with any form of worldly suffering, because you "know" it isn't real. This remoteness will probably feel comfortable and good, because it's the way your ego mind already prefers to do business. So the ego has managed to co-opt your very sincere practice of Oneness to promote more of its own brand of separation.

On the other hand, the flipside will bring exactly the same result. If your heart bleeds for the plight of the underdog, you probably find it very hard to look away from evidence of injustice or suffering. Merely telling yourself it isn't real doesn't help you stop identifying with the pain of the victims. You might sincerely struggle with this aspect of non-dual teaching because you find it unsatisfying and unfair. You'll likely go on volunteering or sending money or marching in demonstrations as you did before.

Yet you really do want to believe the practice of Oneness ultimately brings an end to all suffering, so you maintain an uneasy blend of faith and action, never quite reconciling the two.

The underlying problem is the same for you as for your emotionally removed counterpart. You still very much believe on an unconscious gut level that you're a distinct individual living inside a real body in a world chock-full of other real bodies. And that means your tendency to judge and find others guilty of transgression against helpless victims—which is very much your ego mind's way of promoting its own agenda—only ends up strengthening your belief in separation.

It's tricky, I know.

Personally, I fall a bit into both camps. I am largely unmoved when confronted with some forms of pain, yet feel the siren call of activism at other times, depending on the cause. So I know what both of these tendencies are made of. I can tell you there are no one-size-fits-all answers on this subject; only you can find a way of operating in the world that works for you.

This much seems clear: Our job is not to get hooked into the world's unconscious stories as we witness the suffering. If you're the righteous activist, that means your work is to examine and dismantle your desire to right the world's wrongs. There's a boatload of unconscious ego crap hiding within that mindset, trust me. Feel free to reach out and continue to alleviate worldly pain while you're at it, of course. But Job One is to find a way to care for others without strengthening your own belief in separation.

And you, Ivory Tower Person. If you harbor an honest interest in becoming permanently awakened to truth, sooner or later you're going to have to get your hands dirty like everybody else. The muddy bricks of your casino aren't going to dismantle themselves.

Again, I'm not saying there's anything wrong with intellectualized Non-Dualism *or* passionate activism. Knock yourself out. Really.

I'm just saying unless you're sincerely willing to do the work of examining and releasing all the deeply held egoic stuff that lies beneath your personal attitudes and assumptions, any hope of enlightenment will remain indefinitely out of reach.

THE DINNER PARTY

Funny, the way self-inquiry sometimes works. Now that I've gotten the ball rolling by consciously asking myself questions, the process seems to continue whether I'm making the effort or not.

A while ago, I threw a little Indian dinner party. I spent most of that afternoon prepping for it. About an hour into it, I was standing at the kitchen counter chopping ginger when I suddenly woke up into myself and asked, *Do I still enjoy doing this?*

It wasn't a complaint, and no preconceived answer sat behind it. The question arose spontaneously and was entirely neutral—just asking.

It surprised me, and I really had to stop and think. Food was no small subject for me. I'd always associated food with love; in fact, that was one of the deepest and most painful areas of unconscious darkness I had yet to clean up. There were so many tangled strands of self-loathing, guilt, pleasure and fear all hooked together inside that mess, that I'd never been able to effectively start the unraveling process before this. It wasn't for lack of trying.

Anyway, the sometimes-compulsive desire to feed my friends and loved ones had always been a supercharged topic. So when the question bubbled up of its own volition, it sort of short-circuited me for a second. I felt a little stab of fear as I stood blinking, bits of ginger stuck to my knife. I wasn't sure I was ready for the answer, whatever it might be.

No, I don't still enjoy it, I concluded after a few moments. Or, to be more precise, I realized cooking for loved ones no longer fed my unconscious needs in quite the same way it used to. To my surprise, this was not a big deal.

I stood looking at my knife awhile longer. *On the other hand,* I thought, *I really don't mind doing it either.* And I went back to chopping aromatics.

The party was great fun; it was good to see everybody. We all laughed 'til we cried as we reconnected and caught up on each others' adventures. But I was standing outside of it the whole time, watching myself dispassionately. And I realized dinner parties no longer nourished me. Not like they used to.

Some small part of me was sad to see this tangled fantasy beginning to dissolve. I knew I would miss my food obsessions when it was time for them to go. But mostly I was relieved.

PART TWO

I'll stop the world
and melt with you

CHAPTER SIX

vision correction
as a daily practice

Several forms of suggested daily practice are outlined in the next portion of this book. I like to lump all of them under the heading of Vision Correction, because (as Spirit once explained to me) all of these exercises are designed to disrupt the ego's view of the world, slowly strengthening our sanity, and restoring our clear vision in the process.

The more often we can perform these vision correction exercises, the more our "eyesight" is healed. And the clearer our vision becomes, the easier it gets to tell the true from the crazy.

WHERE THE RUBBER MEETS THE ROAD

It should be pretty obvious by now that a "church on Sunday" spiritual practice (the kind where it's back to business as usual the moment the last *Amen* has trailed away) is not going to cut it for the Serious Beginner.

What may not be as obvious is this: Even a strong, sincere daily spiritual practice won't cut it either, if the practice is something set apart from everyday life.

If your daily meditation or prayer is surrounded by babbling fountains or the smell of incense, or even just plain, beautiful silence, that's a wonderful thing. I'm not saying it isn't. A respite from your hectic world, a way of recharging your batteries, of connecting with the divine—what could be bad about that? Everybody can use a little break now and then.

And if your practice is also geared toward experiencing those pleasurably transcendent, uplifted states of bliss we talked about earlier, it makes this type of daily discipline doubly welcome as a break from your routine.

But although you might assume some kind of meaningful progress is taking place, this sort of daily spiritual practice remains no more than a hobby, like bungee jumping or skydiving. Like those pastimes, it provides breathtaking moments of freedom, but the minute it's over you'll find yourself earthbound once more.

There's nothing wrong with any of it, as long as you realize this is not where the actual work gets done. Because after that beautiful, transcendent little time-out, you're still heading right back into the dream of separation. And if you leave all that beauty and Oneness behind in the meditation room, only to pick up your life right where you left it half an hour earlier, there really isn't much awakening going on.

You're still going through the motions of a "church on Sunday" kind of practice, only seven times more often.

•   •   •

As Spirit has pointed out to me in no uncertain terms, all the work of waking up must be done in the here and now, while we still believe we live in a 3-D world full of separate minds and separate bodies. It's the moment-to-moment mistakes in perception that make up the fabric of our illusory dream life; the job of waking up is to recognize these mistakes while we're making them, and work to correct the error.

Well actually, I've found there's a very important third step in between those two: Recognizing the error, *choosing to do something about it*, and then working to correct it. Recognizing it is hard, but in my experience, wanting to correct it is often harder.

Sometimes blaming the world around me instead just seems a whole lot more satisfying, even though I know damn well I'm completely mistaken about it. So, I find I sometimes have to wrestle my ego mind to the ground before it will allow the vision correction work to take place. Overcoming that egoic resistance can be a very big job; by comparison, performing the actual vision correction is a piece of cake. At least for me.

Anyway, that's the down-and-dirty, moment-by-moment process of challenging the wrong conclusions we make in our 3-D dream world as they arise. This is the work that weakens the ego's influence over our minds, while simultaneously strengthening and healing our perception.

Can you do that in a pretty place with incense wafting? Of course. I do some of my best vision correction work out in the backyard garden. Birds sing, fish frolic as the waterfall gently burbles in the background. Lovely.

But I also do it in front of my computer, while driving on the freeway, or standing in line at Starbucks. Anywhere I happen to recognize physical or emotional disharmony in myself, I take a moment to back the truck up, and work to correct my own faulty perception of the situation.

Sincere vision correction is not particularly joyous or transcendent, although its aftermath often is. And it will no doubt have to be performed over and over and over again (and then over again some more after that), before you permanently awaken and have no further need of it as a spiritual practice.

Yet if the realization of Oneness is your goal, repeatedly challenging your own mistaken perception through self-inquiry and vision correction is pretty much the only game in town. It's all part of the great deconstruction project, the dismantling of your illusory 3-D dream world.

THE BODY AS TRUTH METER

When I do vision correction work, I go entirely by how it makes me feel. That's my yardstick. And by *feel*, I mean emotional feeling coupled with physical feeling.

In my experience, authentic connection with the divine—even the tiniest glimmer of it—is characterized by a marked 3-D physical sensation of freedom and safety, and the gentlest imaginable peace. It's a feeling I could never replicate on my own, and it feels like nothing produced by this world. So I try to maintain my focus within the meditation or exercise, until all anxiety or jangled nerves or general malaise is replaced by that sense of divine peace. I experience this feeling of serenity and expansion right in the pit of my stomach. Which, probably not coincidentally, is also where I experience the anxiety and discomfort the 3-D world shows me. So I rely on my body—or more specifically, my stomach—as a trusted partner in my spiritual practice.

(Yes, I know. This is obvious anti-Oneness heresy. Bodies aren't real. Yet when push comes to shove, I have to admit I still thoroughly believe they *are* real. And chances are, you do too. Are you unsure about this point? Cut off your toe* and then we'll talk.)

---

*My lawyers would very much like you to know I'm kidding. Please don't actually cut off your own toe. Or anyone else's, for that matter.

The point is, your body (illusory though it may be), possesses its own form of intelligence that bypasses the thinking mind altogether. And that's a good thing, because it means there's nobody clouding the issue with logical argument. Using our thinking minds, we can talk ourselves into or out of just about anything. But to your body, it's much simpler than that: The truth feels good, and false stories hurt. Not just sometimes, but every single time. This means the body can be trusted as a very reliable barometer. In fact, it's an unfailingly accurate truth meter.

And as long as you still believe you're a separate mind housed in an individual body (how's that toe?), you might as well use every tool you're offered to help discern truth from falsehood.

So I find it helpful to pay attention to the way my body feels throughout the day. I don't always notice mental stress as it subtly works to disrupt my tranquility, but I can always feel the resulting unease in my stomach. I know the source of this discordant feeling is my resistance to what is; without realizing it, I've fallen back into the habit of believing my ego mind's version of reality. Understanding this makes it easy for me to change the situation. I stop what I'm doing and initiate some vision correction. And I keep it up until I've replaced that unease with a sense of peace.

Sometimes peace happens right away; other times I have to stick with the vision correction for several minutes until my ego mind stops kicking. Yet I know if I don't give up, I'll make the connection eventually. And yes, it takes practice. Everything worthwhile does.

IN THE WORLD? OR *OF* THE WORLD? – PART II

Speaking of bodies, there's another important question many of us seem to wrestle with, when first confronted with the news that the world is fake and we made the whole thing up.

If illness isn't real and bodies are illusory, should we even bother getting those annual checkups anymore?

Like so many other big questions, this is one each of us must answer for ourselves; there is no single right decision. When I first began to study *A Course in Miracles*, I was taught that both sickness and medicine are cut from the same bolt of fantasy cloth. This news rang a deep bell of recognition.

And in response, I immediately stopped going to doctors. But I was already heading that way before I encountered ACIM. Western medicine had failed me badly. And alternative medicine, while highly effective, was such an expensive pain in the ass that I'd burned out on it completely, a number of years earlier. This new information about sickness and medicine really just gave me a firm excuse to do what I already had been doing.

But these days, my attitude is more nuanced. For better or worse, this is the body that accompanies me on my journey. I've begun to see it more as a partner than an annoying reminder that I'm still fooled by the lies my ego mind feeds me.

I don't always get it an annual physical (although I would, if it seemed warranted), but I was on the phone pronto to the dentist, the day after chipping my tooth. I knew the chip was illusory, but it was scratching my imaginary tongue to bits. I accepted the dentist's false remedy gladly.

And if my body is asking me very plaintively for something—more broccoli, or fewer late nights in front of the computer—I will probably try to accommodate it. After all we've been through together, I feel a sort of fond tenderness for this silent sidekick that travels with me through my 3-D existence.

Like those other pesky questions on how to interact with the illusory dream world, the answer seems to be: Don't get hooked into believing bodies or sickness are real. They aren't. But if your body does get sick (and if that sickness persists even after you've sternly informed it of its unreality), then maybe just be grateful for modern medicine. And go remedy your illusory symptoms.

Or don't. Don't take my advice or anybody else's on this. Do whatever feels best for you.

SELF-INQUIRY – PART I

Self-inquiry is essential to the Serious Beginning. But between you and me, it's a pretty harsh tool when used on its own. In my opinion, self-inquiry as a solo method is sort of like a wrecking ball studded with blowtorches. Effective? You bet.

Yet it seems to me there are plenty of ways to dismantle a casino, and I tend to favor a somewhat gentler, more methodical approach in deconstructing mine. But maybe that's just me. If you enjoy that whole personal Armageddon business, stick with self-inquiry exclusively. You won't be disappointed. For the rest of us, there are safer and saner options to choose from.

In my experience, combining rigorous self-inquiry with other forms of vision correction results in a smoother, more balanced process of deconstruction. In the next chapter we'll go into some pretty extensive detail about those other forms of vision correction, because all of them overlap and can be blended together as you choose.

THAT'S ENTERTAINMENT

My advice to anyone contemplating the path of the Serious Beginner is pretty much the same thing they say to people who want to pursue poetry as a full-time career: Only do it if you can't *not* do it.

If the desire for truth is welling up within you, pushing its way out to a degree that can no longer be ignored—well by that time I guess the choice isn't yours to make anymore, is it? Your path is already unfolding, with or without your consent; you might as well get on board.

I would discourage the casual hobbyist, only because the dismantling process can't help but cause some collateral damage along the way. Other people can get hurt.

•　　•　　•

Kurt and I recently celebrated our twentieth wedding anniversary. Although I barely resemble the person he married, he is, astonishingly, supportive of the wholly unexpected turn my life has taken over the past several years. Yet his approval of the big picture doesn't make the small stuff any less difficult to reconcile as the sand shifts beneath our feet.

Take movies, for example. While our tastes in film have never been identical, we've had no difficulty finding common ground. Yet these days, I find my interests are getting narrower all the time. I'm no longer into escapist fare, particularly the epic stories of good triumphing over evil.

Case in point: A couple of years ago we went to see *Avatar* on the big screen. Beautifully made, to be sure. Yet afterward I felt polluted—exhausted from the work of once again watching the ego's favorite timeworn tale of guilt versus innocence. I'm no longer entertained by that story. It isn't fun anymore. I don't want to eat popcorn in the dark and give in to this kind of make-believe.

But Kurt does.

It's in these everyday instances of shifting priorities and opposing desires that it pays to be kind. My advice to anyone facing similar circumstances: Go see the movie or don't; it really doesn't matter. But either way, this is the time to turn off the blowtorches and do your best to honor the people around you. That's how I see it, anyway.

A Serious Beginning is a strictly solo journey, yet for now I choose to make that trip while continuing to walk alongside the loved ones who have accompanied me this far.

And the demolition work goes on, but gently. As carefully as possible, I dislodge each brick before restacking them all in neat piles for recycling.

CHAPTER SEVEN

forgiveness and joining

FORGIVENESS

Forgiveness is the vision correction method recommended by *A Course in Miracles*. This is not forgiveness in the traditional sense. The usual 3-D world version of forgiveness actually reinforces our belief in separation. We see somebody doing a bad thing, and we say: *I judge that you are guilty. Your sins are real. Yet I'm a big enough person to show you mercy in spite of what you did.*

This form of forgiveness causes us to buy into the ego's version of events. We believe the story of guilt is real and we stand apart to attack and condemn, which perpetuates our "us versus them" view of the world. The ego's thought system remains unchallenged.

True forgiveness is designed to do the opposite. True forgiveness means dismissing the false story of guilt the world is showing you. In doing this, you acknowledge you perceive the story incorrectly. You recognize that your mind sees guilt where none exists, so you make the choice to disregard your own faulty ego interpretation. And instead, you consciously try to remember the essential perfection of Oneness that is our shared true nature.

Here's an example of how the forgiveness process might work:

Someone behaves badly and this upsets you. Instead of reacting negatively in response (or, more likely, *after* reacting negatively in response), you would recognize your error and correct yourself by silently saying something to this effect:

Although I'm tempted to perceive you as a total jerk and find you guilty of wrongdoing, in reality I'm completely mistaken about what I think I see in you. I'm not perceiving you as you really are in truth. In truth you are entirely innocent. You are perfect and eternal. You are One with all that is.

This is just a general outline of how a forgiveness exercise might go. Feel free to be spontaneous and creative with it, as the Spirit moves you. All things, people and situations can be forgiven, both currently and retroactively. Anything that disrupts your peace and causes you to buy into your ego mind's version of reality is fair game for forgiveness.

The miraculous thing about forgiveness is this: Because we're all One in truth, the healing we direct outward at illusory "others" is simultaneously received within our own mind. You may think you're forgiving somebody else "out there," (and you are) but in truth you're really forgiving yourself. This self-forgiveness causes beautiful chain reactions of healing on the deepest unconscious levels of your own mind, and in ways you can't predict.

This is a particularly ingenious form of vision correction. The condemnation we're routinely spewing outward at "others" is really being heaped upon ourselves. There are no others. There's only One of us in truth, so every time we attack somebody or something "out there," in truth we're only attacking ourselves. Outward forgiveness relies on the same principle as outward attack, but instead of more suffering it brings the forgiver release from pain, and ever-increasing peace and right-mindedness in its wake.

As with any form of vision correction, the more sincerely you can manage to perform these exercises, the more effective their healing abilities will be. I was very fortunate to be shown this principle firsthand: I experienced the perfection of the "other guy" in a handful of powerful revelatory visions, back when I first began to study ACIM. These visions left me with an indelible sense of what sincere forgiveness feels like.

I wrote about some of these revelatory episodes in *Long Time No See*; the strongest of these visions concerned a guy who had seemed to attack me without provocation, accusing me of all sorts of dark motives, while I was trying to buy a barbeque grill from him on eBay. Although he later apologized for his behavior, after getting my hands on the grill I wanted nothing further to do with him.

Of course, Spirit had other plans. This is the way I described what I was shown at the time:

Later that night, lying in bed I could feel a powerful lesson waiting in the pipeline, something I was supposed to learn about this guy. I knew it was time to stop resisting it.

"Ok, all right. Show me what this Grill Guy is really," I said to Spirit.

Suddenly I was transported.

It was night. I was standing high on a hill, gazing down into a valley obscured by dark, brooding clouds. I could hear the ominous sound of bombs going off in the distance and saw patches of cloud briefly lit from beneath by the explosions. I felt a sense of foreboding; it was obvious I had entered a war zone.

I seemed to glide down the hill and into the valley, and as I did so I saw to my surprise that there were no bombs. The clouds themselves were producing those harmless noises and flashes of light. Beneath the cloud cover, no violence was taking place.

And then I saw it. There, maybe fifty feet in front of me, a slender column of the sweetest, gentlest and most welcoming light imaginable, reaching up through the blackness toward Heaven. I found it irresistible; without conscious intention I moved toward it and merged with it, not noticing until afterward that the whole valley and all its cloud cover had completely vanished, leaving only that perfect Heavenly light.

This is what the Grill Guy is really, said Spirit.

Words fail me when trying to describe the feeling associated with that Heavenly light. Nothing in this world is remotely similar to its beauty and perfection, so words like sweet or peaceful or gentle are hollow stand-ins at best. That light included within it the release from all pain; it was effortlessly strong and unchanging and utterly impartial. I felt it physically in my stomach.

Typically the feelings or realizations associated with revelatory visions fade after a few days. (My theory is it's because I'm only being shown the sensation of divine perfection as a learning tool—I'm not, as yet, actually capable of experiencing the welcoming beauty of that perfection under my own steam.)

This Grill Guy vision is different. It happened several years ago, yet with a little effort I can still conjure at least a partial memory of what that column of light felt like. So I use that memory every time I perform a forgiveness exercise. I fix the person, place or thing in my mind and pause until I can clearly feel the Grill Guy's divine light within my body. I acknowledge wordlessly that the light and the object of my forgiveness exercise are one and the same. Sometimes that's enough; forgiveness exercises don't have to be verbal. Other times (like when I'm seriously bugged by the forgivee, for instance), I like to add in the verbal affirmations of innocence and perfection and all the rest, until my annoyance is eventually replaced by a genuine feeling of peace. I play it by ear.

Not everyone has a Grill Guy vision to fall back on, of course. Yet I've found it helps a great deal to bring a feeling of divine truth into my forgiveness exercises. So my suggestion is to think back to your most sublime, most transcendent moments when you've felt genuine glimmers of Oneness—of authentic love for humanity. Find those moments in your memory, and cultivate them. Try to remember how that felt. And then take that feeling with you into your forgiveness exercises. I really find it helps make an already powerful exercise even moreso.

I should back up and explain here that this form of vision correction is not accomplished alone. The aforementioned higher power is an essential partner in all this. Forgiveness works as it does because it operates according to the truth of Oneness.

As long as you and I still believe we're individual bodies with separate minds, we can't help but deny the reality of the One mind united. Therefore, we're not capable of performing the simultaneous healing of our own unconscious mind that comes as the result of offering forgiveness to somebody else's mind.

But that higher power is entirely capable of it. As we let go of our mistaken perceptions one by one, Spirit (who knows all minds are joined as One) acts on our behalf to correct our vision and bring simultaneous healing to all concerned.

•　　•　　•

Left to our own devices it's difficult, or maybe impossible, to get at our own deepest unconscious ick so we can undo the false perception that holds it in place—precisely because the ick *is* buried deep in the unconscious. How can we hope to dismantle something if it's lurking so far down that we don't even realize it's there?

Yet the roundabout method of vision correction that takes place through forgiveness (healing directed outward at others, which simultaneously heals ourselves) manages to work on the deepest possible levels.

I will share with you a personal example of just how profoundly forgiveness can help bring about the healing of deeply held unconscious pain:

First, a brief bit of background. I began life in this world with the mistaken belief that I was poisonous. And untrustworthy. And a murderer. Later I added shamefully ugly and abnormal and stupid to that list. And I was pretty sure the universe hated me and wanted me dead.

Long Time No See, although ostensibly a chronicle of my spiritual experiences, is really all about that deeply mistaken set of early ideas that formed my perception of myself in this life. Those mistaken ideas went deeper than bone; they seemed to be the very building blocks of my DNA.

This self-hatred and shame manifested in lots of different ways; one of them is that I was ridiculously afraid of strangers. I couldn't stand to let people look at me—their gaze hurt my skin. Add to this an obsessive need for privacy. The thought of anyone, let alone strangers, knowing anything at all about my personal stuff was almost too much to bear.

Oh, and according to various visions I'd been shown, an unresolved past-life trauma was also contributing to my need to hide from the public eye: A long time ago, my private spiritual practices were apparently exposed publicly...and let's just say it ended badly. And five hundred years later I was still carrying around deep residual paranoia at the thought of speaking openly on spiritual matters.

All in all, you could say I was not too fond of the limelight, in this lifetime or any other.

So when Spirit said to me, as casually as if it were reading off yesterday's headlines, *When you're ready, you'll write books*, I was fairly taken aback. Especially since Spirit supplemented these words by simultaneously showing me a vision of Eckhart Tolle standing on a stage, addressing a room full of people.

(I knew I was being shown this vision so I wouldn't get the wrong idea; all my life, I'd had a vaguely romantic notion that writing books would be the ultimate dream job for a recluse like me—I could go live in a cabin by myself somewhere, banging out manuscripts on one of those vintage manual typewriters, and never have to speak to a soul. Just slide the finished manuscripts out under the door and let them make their own way in the world. Ha! Not.)

Anyway. So, against all my instincts and preferences, I agreed to write very personally revealing spiritual books and then speak about them publicly. Onstage, while strangers looked at me. (Well, I wasn't seriously going to say no to the friggin' *Memory Of God In Me*, was I?)

Yet, as I discovered, agreeing to go public and actually accomplishing it were two entirely different things. Agreeing was only the first step. A whole lot of vision correction would have to go down before that could even begin to happen.

•   •   •

During the writing of *Long Time No See*, I found it painful to tell my own stories. I felt intense shame throughout the three-year writing process, and was convinced the book was crap and no one would like it or be able to identify with it. Imagine my surprise when, within a few days of the book's release, I found out just how wrong I was on all counts.

Yet half a year before *Long Time No See* was ever released, I was still struggling hard with the idea of becoming a public figure. I was consumed with fear of what people would think, and couldn't get beyond the terror of being attacked publicly. The thought of finishing the book had me paralyzed, so I kept pushing back the release date.

I knew I needed to dip a toe into the world of social media (ugh) and begin putting myself out there. It was time to start building a community of like-minded souls, and let them know this shameful, stupid book would be coming out soon.

So I opened a Twitter account. And although I may have mentioned spirituality in my personal bio, it was only a whispered aside.

What happened next was later documented in a three-part blog post (yes, I also reluctantly began blogging right about this same time) in July of 2009. Allow me to retell some of it here:

It all started in mid-May, with a workshop Fran was putting on in Philadelphia. Her very first one. Naturally I had to be there.

(If you've read Long Time No See, *you've met Fran as the spiritually gifted Southwestern rock climber. The other half of the story is her previous East Coast society life on Philadelphia's historic Main Line. She's thoroughly at home roughing it in hardscrabble desert backcountry—but you should see her in a pair of Manolos and a little black dress.)*

Anyway, this workshop was a big step for her, for a couple of reasons. First, it took place entirely inside a downtown office building, with a whole bunch of people planted in chairs and waiting expectantly to hear something spiritually helpful. That's quite different from the powerful work she usually performs out in nature, where the land itself becomes a conduit for spiritual connection.

And, second, she was forced to admit to a group of strangers what she really "does," meaning she had to let them in on what her spiritual gifts are, and how those gifts affect the way she sees the world. She'd never done that before; had always been terrified of trusting others with this potentially dangerous information. I can certainly sympathize. But I knew it was what she was being called to do.

She began the day with an overview and a lecture on

quantum science and spirituality—and it was a fascinating lecture, beautifully given—but we both knew she wasn't really connecting. This wasn't it.

During the lunch break she kept asking for my honest assessment of how the workshop was going, so I finally told her: "You need to be authentic and tell these people who you really are and what you really do."

After lunch, she resumed the lecture but right away her attention began to be dragged to one person's thoughts, someone who seemed to have urgent unspoken questions that begged to be acknowledged. Typically, Fran would've resisted this pull, telling herself she had to continue with the lecture as planned, because that's what a "normal" workshop presenter would do.

I was so pleased to see her make the decision to interrupt the lecture and tell everyone the truth of what was happening. She then asked the woman to speak.

In that moment, it all came together. The woman aired her questions; in trusting herself and her connection to Spirit, Fran was able to pull in all sorts of synchronicities that shed new light on the woman's painful situation. The information flowed freely, causing beautiful ripples of secondary healing for several other workshop participants as well. And when it was all over, everyone present that day knew they'd been a part of something extraordinary.

We all agreed Fran's workshop had been a complete success, and I was genuinely thrilled for her. But I knew damn well that when I had told her, You need to be authentic and tell these people who you really are and what you really do, I was actually talking to myself.

I know I'm incredibly fortunate to have the advantage of direct communication with Spirit; I've been told many times in no uncertain terms (both by Spirit and by Fran, who sometimes functions as Spirit's spokesmodel) exactly what my Earthly role and purpose are supposed to be.

I just didn't want to do any of it. At least not yet. Maybe later—you know, after I'm more enlightened or something.

But on my last night in Philadelphia (aided strongly by Fran's "spiritual conduit" effect on me whenever she's nearby) I knew it was time to finally accept the Earthly role and purpose, and just get on with it already. Time to stop dragging my feet. Time to make the quantum leap from terrified shadow-dweller to center-stage truth-teller.

All it would take, really, was a shift in intention. That, and a complete personality transplant.

I decided to make that seemingly impossible leap of faith right then. No matter what it took. And no matter what kind of spiritual work I'd have to do to accomplish it. Sad. Happy. Painful. Scary. It really didn't matter.

All this prayer and intention-shifting was taking place late at night in my darkened bedroom at Fran's house. The moment I put that rock-solid intention out into the universe, some part of my ego mind attempted instant self-sabotage. I'd always been terrified of the supernatural; I watched now as an apparition started to form itself in the dark and move toward me.

Ooh. Scary.

In the past, that's all it would've taken to make me back down and go diving beneath the magic covers for protection, my big, brave vow forgotten. Because even though I was no longer terrified of the supernatural as I used to be, I didn't exactly want it crawling into bed with me, either.

But this time, I just calmly watched as it approached, and then I said: "Bring it. Whatever it takes, I'm ready."

As it turned out, facing that apparition without fear was all it took. The entity, whatever it was, hesitated for a moment and then faded away to nothing. Score one for me, zero for ego-inspired obstacles.

Anyway. My vow to "get on with it already" (that whole Earthly role and purpose thing) newly made, I left Philadelphia the next morning and headed for home. And within a day or two of arriving back in California, I was contacted by this guy on Twitter.

Perhaps "contacted" is not really the word for it. He reached out through the Twitterverse, grabbed my full attention and became an unregulated, unfiltered spiritual conduit, dumping massive quantities of direct Heavenly communication my way.

It was beautiful beyond description.

Naturally he had no idea he was doing it; the supplier of that kind of spiritual linkup is usually the last to know. The event went on for over two weeks, and it was way too much of a good thing. A lot like being hit continuously with a Heavenly fire hose.

I spent hours each day in anguished prayer—repeating fervent forgiveness exercises over and over again—just to keep from drowning in it. If I sound like I'm complaining… well I guess I sort of am. Although it was glorious in concept and sometimes wonderful in actual fact, the overall episode was pretty painful.

(The divine communication itself was perfect, pure, gentle, thoroughly impartial and completely loving. How could it have been anything else? But I wasn't able to absorb such overwhelming nonstop light, so I experienced the gap between my own human need for darkness and that limitless Heavenly radiance as intense emotional pain. I know. Bummer.)

Anyway, after at least ten days of letting me flail around in complete confusion (and more than a little humiliation over this peculiar, one-sided ecstatic experience that I was/was not sharing with a total stranger), Twitter Guy finally admitted this sort of thing happens with him all the time.

He is, in his own words, a "catalyst for other peoples' explosive awakenings." The operative word here being "explosive."

What was this explosive awakening like, you ask? Like somebody dropped a brick building on me. And everything that was fragile got smashed.

After it was finally over I spent another month or so despondently sorting through the rubble. Through it all, I kept up the hours and hours of daily forgiveness work; it was the only thing that brought me any relief.

Then one day I suddenly realized: Hey, I'm not scared anymore. I don't mind if people find out about me. And I don't really care about hiding in shadows, either.

I think I might even be ready for that Earthly role and purpose thing.

So I changed my Twitter username from @carrietriffet to @unlikelymesngr the same day, as a first tentative step out of the spiritual closet. And the rest, as they say, is history.

•　　•　　•

I consider this to have been an authentic awakening experience, even though it had little in common with the first one. What they both shared was the desperate egoic desire to hide in darkness when confronted with unlimited Heavenly light.

Yet unlike that first episode back in 2005, this time I was carrying forgiveness in my tool belt. I was using it mostly for solace, but that didn't seem to matter. I got solace and a whole lot more besides. Looking back, it's a bit hard to say how much of that miraculously deep healing was the result of the Heavenly light blast, and how much was due to the concentrated forgiveness work I put in. At the time, I felt it was mostly the forgiveness work that caused the lasting changes. The blinding light illuminated that which needed healing, and the forgiveness work accomplished it. That's what it felt like, anyway. So you can understand why I remain a big fan of forgiveness as a primary form of vision correction.

(Oh, by the way, that whole "Eckhart Tolle on a stage" thing… well that part's been harder. When it came to public speaking, the desire to hide remained very strong. I was now comfortable with allowing strangers to know my business. And writing was no longer difficult for me; there was no more shame in it. But clearly I still had work to do.)

Anyway, back to forgiveness: I find it lends balance, strength and a very welcome dose of divine gentleness to what can otherwise be a pretty harsh process of waking up. You needn't be a student of *A Course in Miracles* to practice forgiveness, by the way. Whether you feel drawn to study ACIM's teachings or not, the principles underlying forgiveness remain equally true, and will still work beautifully on their own.

I personally consider forgiveness an indispensable complement to the uncompromising nature of self-inquiry. It may seem like a contradiction to advocate a practice that brings deep healing on a 3-D level, if we're trying to dismantle everything about the 3-D world. But deep healing is required for awakening, because as long as we hold onto unconscious pain of any kind, we'll never be able to choose against the dark stories our ego minds are perpetually whispering, just out of earshot.

JOINING

This form of vision correction works to heal the split mind by pointedly ignoring the supposed reality of separation. A joining exercise causes you to temporarily experience the opposite of what your ego mind is telling you about your world.

Joining is bound to be uncomfortable at first, and might remain so for a long time, because it hits the ego right where it lives. Your ego mind, after all, is completely invested in separation. It's not likely to be too happy when it sees you trying to put those broken pieces back together. I say all this with good reason, because joining did not exactly come easily for me.

In fact, I found the whole idea of joining kind of horrifying when Spirit first suggested it. But even after I started doing it and realized for myself the value of this exercise, joining remained unpleasant and hard. I made a point of practicing it now and then despite my distaste for it, but it took at least three years of on-again, off-again attempts before I began to actually enjoy the process.

Now it's my favorite thing to do. And what started as an occasional, peripheral exercise has grown to become the centerpiece of my whole practice of vision correction. On its own, joining is wonderful; combined with anything from self-inquiry to forgiveness to non-judgment, it's even better.

•   •   •

The first time Spirit suggested joining was during a 2006 visit to the Sequoias. I described the incident in detail in *Long Time No See*, but I want to take this opportunity to break it down further to give you a window into my initial egoic reaction. I do this to demonstrate just how resistant I was at first—in case your ego responds to this joining idea the same way mine did.

Spirit broached the subject this way:

Try setting aside all your beliefs about bodies right now. See Kurt hiking the trail up ahead of you? You could take this opportunity to perceive him as perfect divine light and love. Why not leave your body awareness and join together with him and with Me as one immortal holy spirit? Just for a little while?

The suggestion struck me as ludicrous. In fact, this whole topic of conversation was deeply annoying to my ego mind; it felt like someone was scraping sandpaper back and forth across the surface of my brain.

The idea of leaving my own body awareness seemed offensive, outrageous—maybe even downright dangerous. And to then be asked to merge my temporarily homeless awareness with that of another person? Alarmingly inappropriate. Way too intimate.

It was totally unfair of Spirit, I decided angrily, to ask me to put myself in such a vulnerable position.

Besides, I wasn't about to join with anybody as impure and untrustworthy as Kurt. (This was my husband of sixteen years we were talking about. A guy who'd done nothing in this world that was noticeably untrustworthy or impure, by the way.) In response to Spirit's invitation, I was ferocious in my adamant refusal to mingle my awareness with anyone so unsavory:

"Because he doesn't deserve it," I snarled vehemently.

It can be eye-opening to watch the behavior of an ego mind when it feels cornered. True attitudes are swiftly revealed, ripping away the thin veneer of affection and loyalty that passes for love in this world.

Spirit gently corrected me: *You're so wrong. Divine love is what he is.*

In the tranquil light of this statement, I had no choice but to conclude my ego logic had been false. But that breach of egoic perception, however slight, could not be tolerated for even a second. So I instantly turned the tables, bringing the same damning accusation against myself instead:

"Well then, because *I* don't deserve it."

And in that moment I very much meant it; Kurt may have been perfectly pure, but that meant I was far too corrupt and filthy to be allowed to contaminate him with my despicable awareness.

If I couldn't push the guilt onto Kurt and make him the enemy, then I'd do it to myself. When an ego mind is threatened, it really doesn't care who it throws under the bus. Ultimately, it's only looking out for itself.

Spirit, of course, was having none of it: *Again, quite wrong*, it informed me gently. *Divine love is what you are.*

And so began my years-long dance of discomfort with joining. Many times after that, Spirit would suggest joining as an exercise; sometimes with itself, sometimes with other people. It explained we were repeating these exercises over and over so we could wear down my ego mind's resistance to the truth. Building up those sanity muscles, so to speak, to one day help overturn the thought system of separation that makes my 3-D dream world go round.

THE BASICS OF JOINING

All of the joining exercises that follow have been directly suggested to me by Spirit. I'll describe them here for you in more or less the chronological order in which I received them. These are barebones descriptions only, meant to illustrate the point of the exercise along with the general idea of how each meditation might go. I'm leaving all the details to you.

The first method is the way Spirit originally suggested it be done. It sounds hard, and in my experience, it was. But I'm including it here, because it came direct from the horse's mouth so I want to give you the option if you feel inspired to try this version.

JOINING WITH ANOTHER PERSON

Begin a meditation in which you focus only on your own conscious awareness, allowing your body awareness and your thinking mind to recede into the background. Remind yourself (non-verbally if possible) that this conscious awareness is what you really are.

Try to recognize this awareness of your essential self as pure and eternal. Stay focused on these qualities until you distinctly feel a sense of peace in your body as you connect with your own pure, eternal nature.

Now bring the other person to mind. Look beyond their personality, their body and everything they've ever done in this world. Focus only on the shining purity of eternal awareness that is the essence of their being. It is made of exactly the same stuff as the essence of your being. Stick with this awareness until you authentically begin to feel the same purity in their nature as you feel in your own.

Once you've managed this to whatever degree possible, bring your awareness of self and awareness of the other person side by side. Do your best to drop all egoic resistance, and gently try to merge both awarenesses until they become one. Focus on this single combined awareness for as long as you can manage.

Did I mention how hard this is? In the beginning I found it physically uncomfortable—in my entire body, not just the stomach—and mentally intolerable. We're talking jumpy legs and twitchy skin, combined with an acute annoyance comparable to nails on a blackboard.

Yet there are worlds of peace and healing to be found here, if you're willing to stick with it long enough to get beyond your ego mind's initial resistance.

JOINING WITH SPIRIT

This is much like joining with another person, except of course there's no need to overlook the body or past misdeeds of the other.

Recognize the purity of your own essential nature, then feel the essence of Spirit's perfection. Bring the two side by side, and allow your own awareness to melt into the Oneness that is Spirit. Let your sense of a separate self disappear as completely as you can, and focus only on the One self.

Do this for as long as possible.

THE JOINING POOL

This joining meditation was suggested to me a few years after the first one; I like it because I find visualization sometimes helps make the joining process a little easier. This exercise is especially valuable if there's something or someone troubling you in your 3-D world, because it acknowledges the illusory problem before asking you to leave it behind.

Visualize a circular cavern. It's large and clean and airy feeling. A sparkling pool of water is found at the center of the cavern. That pool of water is your Source, and it's infinitely deep. You feel good just looking at it.

If you've brought specific worries into this cavern with you, take one last look at them and then dump that baggage by the side of the pool; there's no need to bring it beyond this point. Your Source knows what all your illusory troubles are. You're free to release them now.

Dive into the pool.* As you do so, make your body water-soluble. Feel the cells of your bones, muscles, organs and skin filling with water and gradually dissolving away until only your thinking mind and awareness remain.

Now relax the boundaries of your thinking mind. Let its edges soften, visualizing the water as it gently fills up the thinking mind and slowly dissolves it as well.

*For years I used to get hung up on what I was supposed to be wearing during these kinds of visualizations of myself. If you're prone to similar meditation obstacles, I'll make the decision for you: Tee shirt and jeans. And they dissolve away instantly along with the rest of you, as soon as you enter the water.

Now you're nothing but pure awareness. Let your awareness lose all characteristics of individuality, merging completely with that perfect water. Stay in this formless state as long as possible.

If another person is troubling you, you can bring them with you to the cavern to join with you and with your shared Source. Leave the specifics of your grudge or pain by the side of the pool, then throw this person into the water before you jump in yourself.

Did I say throw? I meant gently invite.

Apply all the steps mentioned above to both yourself and the other person, merging your own awareness and theirs with the Source pool as thoroughly as you can for as long as you can. Stay together in this shared state until you recognize the telltale signs of peace within your body.

I love the joining pool meditation. Nowadays I don't always bother with the pool-and-cavern imagery; I just look within to locate that infinitely deep Source, then I quickly dissolve the meat suit and go straight into joining. I can take these shortcuts because after having practiced the pool meditation so many times, I know what each of the steps feels like when done properly. So I seek to replicate those feelings, if not necessarily the steps that originally produced them. It's a great timesaver.

THE JOINING POOL AS A MICRO-MEDITATION

Actually, I'm not joking about the time savings. Recently I started doing micro-meditations—once every hour I'll take a break in my 3-D life to stop whatever I'm doing and join with Source as described on the previous page, for anywhere from thirty seconds to a couple of minutes.

There's no magic formula in my decision to do this hourly; I just happen to live up the block from a church, so I hear the church bells as they chime on the hour. It's an easy reminder to stop and join.

My ego mind hates this regimen, naturally. Even though these exercises are short and sloppy, the commitment to remember Oneness a dozen times a day or more is deeply threatening to the ego. This is because awareness of Oneness becomes a part of the fabric of daily life. My dream state gets interrupted by truth commercials every hour on the hour. No wonder the ego feels threatened.

Once you've mastered the mechanics of joining, I highly recommend an occasional regimen of these hourly micro-meditations. You probably won't be able to keep it up for long; the first time I tried it, I managed fewer than two days' worth of hourly interruptions before my ego mind basically threw up all over itself. (By that I mean I got a headache; was plagued by insomnia and nightmares; was unable to concentrate; became suddenly twice as busy as before; couldn't remember to do the exercises more than once or twice a day; felt too cranky to care whether I did them or not…you get the idea.)

So if you do decide to try the micros, my advice is: Be gentle with yourself. If an hour comes and goes and you've forgotten to do the exercise, don't beat yourself up. There's another opportunity coming up sixty minutes later. If your boss or your spouse calls you up just as the clock strikes the hour and keeps you on the phone awhile, don't stress. Life will sometimes get in the way, especially if you're trying to keep this routine going during office hours.

And once your ego mind hits the wall (as it surely will), don't bother trying to soldier on anyway. This is a very advanced meditation practice, even though it seems simple and quick at first glance. Let it go, and congratulate yourself for whatever small successes you managed in that first go-round.

Then some other time, after another week or month goes by and you're feeling inspired, try it again. Who knows, maybe it'll be a little easier the next time. Or maybe it won't. Either way, these repetitions will help build those sanity muscles—and you know what they say about muscle-building: No pain, no gain.

In my experience, these micros do get easier with time. In fact, they've become a source of comfort. Now I sometimes make a point of starting an hourly regimen if I know I'm in for a very hectic or stressful workday; although the exercises still irritate my ego mind a bit, all that concentrated joining leaves a deep residue of unshakable peace behind. So much so, that I find the events of my day don't matter much. It's the peace that counts.

JOINING THE ONENESS WITHIN

What follows is one of the most powerful forms of joining meditation I've tried so far, because it symbolically mimics the experience that took place during the Dinner Table Awakening of 2005. I call it "Oneness meets Oneness."

When I'm feeling especially strong and clear, I make this the basis of my hourly micro-meditation practice, at least a few times during the day. (I usually can't manage more than three or four of these in a row.) Any ego mind is guaranteed to hate this one.

ONENESS MEETS ONENESS

Instead of joining with a Source pool that is outside myself, I go inward to find the infinite Source within. I join with it until I feel the activated Source essence within me, staying with it until I firmly feel its limitless peace as a physical sensation in my body.

Next I visualize this joined Oneness of self and Source as being located at the center of the Earth. I stay with it until I feel this location very clearly. Next I inhale deeply, and on the exhale

I allow an unstoppable wave of Oneness to expand outward from the Earth's core. This peaceful wave grows effortlessly, encountering no resistance as it gently engulfs the Earth and races out in all directions through planets, stars and galaxies.

The unstoppable wave of Oneness keeps expanding until it encompasses the entire universe. And then it breaches the outer edges of the universe itself, to reunite with the eternal truth of Oneness that lies beyond.

And as Oneness meets Oneness, eternal truth is immediately recognized as such. And by comparison, the 3-D universe of dreams reveals its unreality, becoming a little thinner, a little less convincing in its attempts to hide the unadulterated truth that has always been.

JOINING WITH THE VOID

Ok, one last joining exercise before we move on. Every so often while meditating or performing vision correction exercises, I experience a sudden lack of egoic resistance, for no particular reason. Suddenly there's no fear, and it's wonderfully easy to focus on the exercise at hand. Maybe that happens now and then for you, too. If it does, this exercise is for that rare moment when the ego mind happens to not be guarding the gate.

Joining with the void is as creepy as it sounds, which is why you should only try this when your ego mind isn't home; it would be far too frightening an exercise to attempt under more typical circumstances.

This form of joining is much like the standard joining exercise; you're in the cavern with the pool—except instead of making the pool your Source, make it the void of no-self. Total undefined emptiness. No divine love, no nothing. Jump in and allow your body and mind to dissolve into that emptiness. Let your awareness become one with the void. Stay there in no-self nothingness for as long as you can.

• • •

Is the return to Oneness really a void? Is there honestly nothing at all, once the "me" self has dissolved away? Good question. I can only speak for my own limited experience.

Far from being a void, on the rare occasions I have managed

to choose it wholeheartedly, no-self has revealed itself to be a very alive awareness, composed of undifferentiated love. Yet there's a catch: It seems no-self is only free to reveal its nature *after* the ego's story has been consciously rejected. There can be no fear present in the mind, while experiencing this loving awareness.

At least that's how it's been for me.

Fear of the void is at the very heart of our unconscious resistance to the truth of all reality. We are terrified that a full return to Oneness means we will cease to exist. In fact, it only means our ego minds will cease to exist. We ourselves are eternal.

So why would I bother recommending a practice of void-centric vision correction, if the void isn't real?

It has only recently become possible for me to embrace no-self without fear; I'm fairly sure this is due to my many prior efforts to embrace the void through joining exercises like the one described here. Maybe the same will be true for you.

THE EGO AS ENEMY – PART II

Gloria Steinem once said: *The truth will set you free. But first it will piss you off.*

This observation brings us back once again to our original ACIM question: Do we want to be right, or happy? I spoke earlier of choosing happy as if it were a no-brainer decision. Yet happiness (AKA truth) requires that we take responsibility for everything that happens in our lives, which means there's nobody "out there" to blame for any of it. And this can be a very tough concept to swallow.

After all, the need to push blame outward runs very deep in all of us. To participate in the 3-D dream world of the ego means we have no choice but to view ourselves as victims of circumstance. We compulsively judge and condemn others for their sins, in order to stand apart and see ourselves as innocent victims. This "us versus them" mindset is part and parcel of separation.

To us, judgment and condemnation seem like the only logical responses to all the nasty stuff we see in the world. Our ego minds have quite a lot invested in perceiving ourselves as innocent victims of outside events; we'd really rather not drop that view and see ourselves as willing self-saboteurs instead.

Some types of egoic self-sabotage seem easier to identify than others. If you're in a situation, for instance, where your mind is working at semi-conscious cross-purposes, chances are you're at least dimly aware this is happening. I'll use a familiar relationship phenomenon to illustrate the point. If you've spent any time at all wading in the dating pool, you're bound to recognize this behavioral pattern as belonging either to you or a partner:

I was dating this person and realized I was starting to have genuine feelings for him/her. That scared me. So I got weird, picked a fight and broke up. That way I could be the one to leave first, before he/she had a chance to reject me.

In this example, it's fairly easy to recognize the destructive influence of our own ego mind at work, as it invents obstacles designed to interfere with our desired outcome of a happy relationship. But what about ego obstacles that *don't* appear to come from our own minds? Do we really have to be responsible for those, too?

•　　•　　•

I had a hard time at first with this business of taking personal responsibility for everything in my world, whether it was clearly my doing or not. It isn't that I particularly wanted to think of myself as a victim. Yet I resented the idea that abstract things like car accidents were supposed to be my own doing. *But that guy ran the red light*, I'd splutter heatedly if anyone tried to point out I willingly chose to have that car crash experience.

It seemed ridiculously unfair that I wasn't supposed to push blame outward anymore, even if something was clearly not my fault. It took more than two decades of spiritual practice before I realized assigning fault and blame made me *more* frustrated and unhappy, not less. And that meant I was finally ready to honestly examine ACIM's question: Would you rather be right or happy? and think to myself, *Oh, I definitely choose happy.*

It took me that many years because it's hard to see the ego's clandestine workings as it shapes our experience of the world. It's even harder to recognize and accept our own limitless powers of unconscious creation. And that means things often happen to us that look as if they're not our own doing. Yet they're *always* our own doing. It couldn't possibly be any other way.

Once again I want to emphasize this point: It may seem from my dire descriptions throughout this book that I think we should all hate the big, bad ego mind for the rotten things it does to us. Not so. The ego mind is only doing your bidding and mine.

Hatred, as we discussed earlier, is an inappropriate response to the workings of the ego mind. What's really called for is the acceptance and understanding that we're actually doing all this to ourselves. Individually and collectively we're in pain on an unconscious level, and unregulated ego havoc is our crazy attempt at pain management.

This is true on a global scale, and it's true for each individual person as well. If you break your leg; if a thief encounters fifty unlocked bicycles and chooses, out of all of them, to steal yours; if a toothache ruins your wedding day—these are all examples of ways your own ego mind is seemingly working to punish you. Yet it's important to remember the ego is only doing what you yourself ask of it. Without exception, responsibility for what you experience is yours alone.

You are the puppet master, sound asleep as you yank mercilessly on those strings. And the chaos you create in your own life and your world is directly proportional to the amount of guilt, pain and self-hatred you feel on an unconscious level.

So Job One for all of us is to dig in and dissolve the guilt and self-loathing that fuel our ego minds. As these unconscious motivators are removed bit by bit, we find we don't need to punish ourselves or "others" quite as much or as often as we did before. As we feed the ego less of this unconscious fuel, our lives automatically become happier and more peaceful. Eventually, starved of nourishment, the ego's power begins to wane and our right mind grows ever-stronger in influence.

This is what vision correction is designed to do.

NIGHT OF THE END OF DAYS

Back in the days of my Buddhist practice, I began to have occasional recurring dreams. Although the details varied, in each of them the main storyline was the same: Because I had pushed my landlord too hard, demanding rights that weren't really mine, I was now forced to move out of my comfortable house and into a smaller, darker, uglier apartment.

These dreams popped up whenever I happened to stumble too close to the ego's propaganda machine. They were always meant as an unsubtle warning to back off—a friendly reminder that all change is bad, and if I persisted in using my spiritual practice to dig for the truth, I'd be sorry. I should just trust in my good friend the ego mind instead; after all, it knew best how to take care of me.

Later, when I started to practice *A Course in Miracles*, the dreams became more direct in their warnings, because my ego mind was starting to feel genuinely threatened. This business of Oneness was not a good thing—didn't I realize joining meant there would be no more "me"? Why, that would be spiritual suicide. Something must be done to protect me from myself.

So my ego employed a new set of recurring dreams. These ones were about identity theft. Night after night, I'd leave my handbag unattended for only a second, and when I looked again I'd find that my wallet was gone. Each time it happened, this loss produced in me a swirling sense of fear and helpless disorientation. It wasn't really about the money; I was gripped with anxiety over the missing driver's license and credit cards. They were my anchors in this 3-D world. Without them, how could I prove I am who I say I am?

These nighttime warnings became that much more insistent once I made the commitment to a Serious Beginning. And I really wasn't surprised; when we're actively engaged in dismantling the ego's thought system, naturally the ego mind isn't going to take it lying down. Bad dreams are one common response. These days, mine often contain cataclysmic warnings to stop the dismantling, or else.

This one I had a while back is typical: I dreamed I was witness to an epic war of the worlds. It was an end of days battle between the good guys—humans of Earth, naturally—and evil, unseen alien forces from outer space.

Most of the dream was filled with terrifying doomsday images of destruction; we poor Earthlings were helpless against the spaceships' omnipotent laser weapons. They killed with blinding light, annihilating everything in their path. And there was nowhere I could run or hide, because the aliens were tracking my every move. They knew what I was thinking even before I did.

(Clearly the faceless "aliens" in this dream were stand-ins for Spirit. Who else would employ brilliant light to destroy the 3-D world, or be privy to my thoughts even before I was? The ego mind traffics in lies and darkness. It perceives truth and light as killers, and is convinced they must be battled at all costs; to the ego, there's no greater enemy.)

Anyway, next I found myself in a huge, empty hall with thirty-foot ceilings. One whole wall of windows was covered by filmy, white floor-length curtains. A spaceship entered the room to search for me; I hid behind the translucent curtain, knowing I was plainly visible. Yet I couldn't help myself. My need to hide in darkness was so strong I had no choice but to try.

The ship aimed its laser and obliterated the hall. I felt my body and mind disintegrate, but my awareness stayed around for a few seconds after that. This event felt unmistakably familiar; it was the same series of sensations found in the joining pool exercise.

Then I woke up. (I don't mean I awakened. I mean I woke up, looked at the clock and realized I'd overslept the alarm by an hour.)

My ego mind had made its point very clearly in this dream: *You say you want awareness instead of everything else? Presto! There you go. Awareness. And in exchange, your whole world destroyed. Happy now?*

I bring this up just to let you know what you can expect if you engage in direct ego-mind confrontation. You may experience some crazy-ass dreams full of dire peril and obvious metaphors, like this one. Or you may not. You might have wonderful dreams instead. Some of the most peaceful, healing dreams I've ever experienced have come since I started questioning everything. My point is, it's all normal. It's all to be expected.

CHAPTER EIGHT

judgment and stories

JUDGMENT AND THE POWER OF BELIEF

The common tendency is to practice Oneness as an intellectual exercise, more than a daily, "get your hands dirty" practice. That's entirely understandable; Non-Dualism is a pretty mind-blowing concept.

Yet as I've pointed out all along, intellectual theory is not really where it's at—beyond the initial absorption of the information, anyway. Our ego minds form mental judgments about everything we see. Part of the healing process our minds undergo is to learn to reject judgment, in order to see the truth that lies beyond it.

The only way to use a practice of Oneness properly, then, is in our moment-to-moment decisions on how to perceive the stories the world shows us: *Do I see this story as unreal, with perfect truth beyond it? Or do I get sucked into making false judgments, believing these tales of guilt and imperfection are real?*

The choice, in actual practice, is not so cut and dried. We drift in and out of both kinds of perception as we work to heal our fractured minds. Yet clinging to Oneness as intellectual theory lends itself to a particularly unfortunate hybrid form of practice. And it doesn't actually do much to help heal the mind (at least not to the degree it might), because it's a fertile ground for even more judgment.

Here's what I mean by that: We are taught that in Oneness, all is perfect and eternal. Separate bodies are not real. Imperfection, sickness and death are not real.

The intellectualized tendency is to take those teachings we have not yet made our own, and spit them all back at the world. A loved one is sick and miserable with the flu; instead of offering Kleenex and compassion, the intellectualizer spanks them for believing in the illusion of sickness.

Yes, it's true the other person is busy believing in illusion. But so is the intellectualizer. So are we all, as long as we believe we're separate individuals capable of standing apart and judging one another.

This whole universe is illusion, if you want to get technical about it. Surely a bad cold is no more or less illusory than our own bodies, our houses, our jobs or the planetary orbit of the Earth around the sun.

Ideally, a practice of Oneness would make us *more* compassionate of "others," not less. But that compassion would be borne of authentic healing, a glimmer of connection to the divine perfection that is our true shared nature. And that authentic connection can only come from doing the everyday drudgework of choosing truth, again and again, instead of the stories the ego mind presents to us.

Truth must be felt; it isn't a mental concept. Intellectual understanding, on the other hand, is real estate owned wholly by the ego mind. Do any of us really want to build our homes there?

•   •   •

Let's talk a bit more about the unfathomable power of our own minds, because it's an important part of this discussion. Although our ego minds flatly deny it, in truth we are limitlessly powerful creators. We can build something out of nothing just by believing in it. The thing we've built isn't part of ultimate truth, of course. It's just a fantasy. But in this 3-D world, if we thoroughly believe (consciously or unconsciously) that something is true and real, we will experience rock-solid evidence that proves it's so. In other words, the thing we believe becomes true and real for *us*.

Let's look at one rather striking example of this phenomenon: According to the teachings of Oneness, there can be no such thing as dark spirits, evil forces or the big red guy, Satan himself. It's all One, and that One is composed only of perfect light and love. This radiant love has no opposite.

Yet, in certain places and certain belief systems, Satan rules. And many people have had authentic, firsthand supernatural experiences of pure malevolent evil. Our own belief is what holds this world and all its phenomena—including the unseen and the supernatural—together. In those aforementioned segments of the population, fearful belief in Satanic forces is strong and so those things exist. 3-D reality is very subjective, and their reality includes the devil.

Let me repeat this, because it's true of all phenomena in our 3-D existence, whether seen or unseen. According to the teachings of Oneness (and specifically ACIM), we are borne of our creator as intrinsic parts of our creator, equipped with full powers and abilities of creation. We are currently misusing those powers of creation to build and sustain this false 3-D playground we call home. It's our ongoing belief in our miscreations that keeps the illusion real for us.

Are our miscreations real in ultimate truth? Nope. But the rule is: If you believe in it here in 3-D, it's thoroughly real for you. So there are folks in this world who are convinced through personal experience that the devil is real. And they're absolutely right—the devil is real *for them*.

So I find myself hanging out with Linda Blair, and her bed is on the ceiling as I'm dodging pea soup and watching her head turn three-hundred-sixty degrees. What do I do? Do I put on my best superior smirk and inform her that her belief system is faulty because Satan isn't real? Oh sure, I'd be technically accurate about that. But she's a little busy right now…so what's my purpose in saying it?

As I watch this Satanic episode unfold, my only task is to choose truth and reject fantasy *for myself.* Correcting somebody else's misperceptions is not part of the job description. Nobody died and made me the judgment sheriff; other peoples' mistaken beliefs are not within my jurisdiction. Besides, intellectual judgment (no matter how well-intentioned) never manages to be authentically kind or helpful to self or others.

To illustrate this point: There's a famous Chinese proverb that says I can give a hungry man a fish and feed him for a day, or I can teach a man to fish and feed him for a lifetime.

According to some intellectual interpretations of Oneness, however, there would be a third option: I could tell that starving man his hunger is not real, because all is perfect in eternal Oneness and lack is impossible. And then I could walk away, smugly satisfied that I helped this man by informing him of his misperception.

Yes, I could totally do that. And I suppose there'd be nothing technically wrong with it. But it sure as hell wouldn't help me awaken any sooner.

THE LINK BETWEEN NON-JUDGMENT AND ONENESS

Judgment is an intrinsic part of the thought system of separation. After all, it's only possible to judge something if you're standing apart from it. Even self-judgment involves the ego mind as witness and commentator as it stands apart to praise or condemn itself.

Judgment is completely alien to the One self; it's a made-up function of the ego mind, and its purpose is to constantly uphold our belief in separation.

To practice non-judgment, then, is to weaken the ego mind's ironclad grip on perception. Practicing non-judgment isn't easy; our brains aren't cut out for it. Everything about the way we perceive and process our world typically involves some kind of judgment. Judgment is automatic to the ego mind. It's like breathing; we even do it in our sleep.

So is judgment necessary for living? Surprisingly, the answer seems to be no. From what I've been shown by Spirit, judgment would mostly be replaced in the fully awakened mind by a deeper trust connection with the One self.

My own experience seems to support this; on those rare occasions when I'm truly tuned into Spirit, moment-to-moment decisions are made, not by employing judgment, but by following the flow of divine inspiration. The thinking mind plays little or no role in this. Even for a fully awakened person, I suspect judgment would still be a handy tool for negotiating life in 3-D—yet unlike the rest of us, they'd never be ruled by a compulsive need to use it.

But that's not how we regular folks operate. We're addicted to our thinking minds, you and me, and judgment makes our world go round. It's almost impossible to avoid participating in it, as long as we're still the willing puppets of our own ego minds.

Yet it seems to me it's worthwhile to try to observe the world—at least now and then—without using judgment to assign meaning. Every time we manage even a moment of non-judgment, it's a significant step toward strengthening our sanity, by rejecting the upside-down fantasy world we call home.

CONNECTING THE DOTS

I wrote a blog post a while back that describes the mechanics of judgment and non-judgment in pretty simple terms, so I will begin this discussion by including parts of that article here:

This is a simple way to describe non-judgment: You have one dot over here and another dot over there. So, through non-judging eyes, what do you see? Two unrelated dots, nothing more.

But that's not how we humans view things. Judgment is the function of our ego minds. We see a dot over here and another one over there, and we automatically connect them. Most of the time we don't even realize we're doing it. We tell ourselves a story that seems to fill up the space between those dots, and that story becomes our truth.

But really, it's a story and nothing more.

Let's look at a hypothetical example of how this works: I see a dog on a street corner. He has no collar. He looks dirty. I automatically say to myself, There is a stray dog.

It's a conclusion I've reached entirely on my own. And because I historically have an affinity for animals and underdogs, I go on to embellish the story further:

He must be hungry and tired, poor thing.

I wonder if he's been abandoned on that street corner.

I'll bet he's waiting for an owner who's never coming back.

People are so cruel.

So I've taken the three dots of "dog on a street corner" and "no collar" and "looks dirty," and I've used it as an excuse to weave a present story that reinforces my own past forms of condemnation onto the world:

I do not forgive you for cruelty to animals.

Just then, the dog's human emerges from the garage of that house on the corner with a tub and a garden hose—and suddenly the story has changed completely.

It's still nothing but a story, mind you, as the dog turns and trots after the person, and they both watch the tub fill with soap and water. Now my story involves a squeaky clean puppy whose collar will be returned as soon as he's dry.

I feel sheepish and ashamed of my earlier wrong conclusion. I attacked that dog's owner for no reason, I think to myself. Clearly, this pup is loved. He's cared for. I made a bad mistake.

I'm still connecting dots, but this time I'm doing it to condemn myself for my own misguided prejudices.

•   •   •

Connecting dots may seem like a harmless pastime, but it isn't. We connect dots constantly, and it's those stories we fabricate that make up the world as we know it. Yet the world *isn't* as we know it. Not by a long shot. We can't begin to know the world's true nature until we stop telling ourselves made-up lies about it.

Our compulsive need to connect dots—to judge random unrelated things and weave stories of good/bad, and right/wrong around them—this is the addiction to judgment that blocks our memory of Oneness.

As long as we go on making judgments, telling ourselves fantasy stories about each other to give our world meaning, we miss this eternal truth: The world *has* no meaning. It's just a whole lot of disconnected dots, signifying nothing.

Yet if we patiently retrain our minds to leave those dots disconnected—to refrain from filling the in-between spaces with our fantasy judgments—that's when the light of Oneness (which is always loving and entirely without judgment of any kind) has room to filter into our awareness.

To practice non-judgment is to see the dots, but to resist the temptation to assign them a meaning they really don't possess.

Everything about non-judgment is hard for ego minds to get used to. It's uncomfortable for us to leave the dots unconnected—we're hardwired for storytelling. But non-judgment is an essential component of a permanently awakened life. It's what they mean when they talk about being *in* the world (walking around still attached to a body, rubbing shoulders with others as you negotiate your daily life) and not *of* the world (believing the stories you see there).

Non-judgment means taking absolutely everything at face value, refusing to connect dots. When we stop weaving stories, it instantly becomes clear the dots themselves are meaningless. This is why all the great wisdom teachings stress the importance of non-judgment.

So it pays to exercise the non-judgment muscles, to try and let go of our need to be right about everything in the world around us. Because we're really not right about anything in the world around us. We have no clue whatsoever about the true nature of the world around us.

●　　●　　●

A few years back, Spirit taught me a profound lesson about non-judgment. I talked about it in *Long Time No See,* but once again, I want to take this opportunity to describe the episode in more detail here.

I had this awful, depressing dream that I couldn't get home from India, spending most of the dream hopelessly lost as I searched in vain for the airport. It was my ego mind's way of assuring me I would never awaken to spiritual truth and be able to "fly home" to Heaven—I'd just drive around in circles instead, stuck forever in search mode.

Toward the end of the dream, I drove into a big warehouse or airplane hangar; people milled about on all sides. As I looked directly in front of me, I saw a very tall A-frame stepladder. Its uppermost rungs held a random assortment of dime store devotional items—little plastic incense burners shaped like your favorite deities, that sort of thing.

As I craned my neck to look up at it more closely, I was surprised to see the ladder itself reached only forty feet or so into the air. And I realized most of these people had never bothered looking up. That ladder had been around since long before they were born, and they just assumed it went all the way up to the sky.

I decided this stepladder was useless to my search, yet I couldn't move past it because my car was too wide to fit between its angled legs. My only solution was to ask the locals to move it aside so I could keep going. (At this point, the alarm clock woke me up.)

A few days later, Spirit interpreted the meaning of this dream for me:

By the way, Spirit asked, *how do you suppose that India dream would've turned out if I'd been in control of the car instead of you? What do you suppose would've happened with that ladder?*

"I don't know the significance of the ladder."

You looked up and saw the top of that ladder, and you saw it didn't reach as high into the sky as the locals assumed it did. And so you judged this erroneous ladder to be blocking your way. You insisted the people move it, even at the risk of causing them offense.

In other words, you thought you perceived the limitations of their spiritual belief system, judged it an unnecessary hindrance to you, and demanded that it be pushed aside so you could pass.

Had I been in the driver's seat, the car would have traveled right through that ladder as we swiftly made our way home.

Nothing is ever truly in your way, dear one. That's the gift non-judgment brings you.

At the time, our conversations had been mostly on the topic of surrender. Much as I wanted to, I was finding it impossible to give up the steering wheel and let Spirit "drive the car," in any aspect of my waking or sleeping life.

So I was a bit surprised when Spirit threw that unexpected zinger about non-judgment into the discussion. I dimly realized the importance of the lesson at the time, although I didn't quite understand its meaning yet. But now, years later, I often think about that statement: *Nothing is ever truly in your way, dear one. That's the gift non-judgment brings you.*

Stated another way: There is infinite freedom to be found in the refusal to connect dots. If I didn't tell myself fixed stories of right/wrong, making automatic judgments of better/worse, or greater/lesser about the world, I would find endless space to maneuver between those meaningless dots. When my need to tell stories goes away, so do all the perceived obstacles in my path.

Non-judgment is closely interrelated with non-resistance. If you're not judging anything, it means everything in this dream world is equally ok. And if everything is fine exactly as it is, what is there to resist? This is the polar opposite, in other words, of how our ego minds interpret the world and everything in it.

•   •   •

What does a practice of non-judgment look like? To use the earlier example of the dirty dog on the street corner, first I catch myself making up stories about the dog, and then I stop doing it.

Yes, just like that. I stop spinning the story, and go back to the only things I actually know about the situation. Scruffy dog. No collar. Street corner. If the story disturbs me (as the abandoned dog scenario did), I combine this exercise with a joining pool exercise. I leave the unconnected dots at the water's edge, and then I jump in and join with Spirit for awhile. The joining soothes and strengthens my mind while I work to keep those dots apart.

If disconnection of dots sounds suspiciously similar to the dismantling of bricks, it should. Non-judgment plays a vital role in self-inquiry. In asking, *what do I know for sure about myself and my world?* our first step is to disregard all the stories and look only at the dots.

But we'll talk more about self-inquiry a little later. Right now I want to discuss another aspect of non-judgment that's worth watching out for. In my ongoing quest to be as careful and kind as possible with self and others as I walk my spiritual path, I offer this next topic in case that's a goal of yours, too.

WHEN EGO MASQUERADES AS SPIRIT

Whenever the ego mind dons the mantle of Spirit, it's never a pretty thing. The spiritual ego is the original wolf in sheep's clothing. It may look warm and fuzzy on the outside, but whenever it's around, somebody is guaranteed to get hurt.

This is not a rare occurrence, by the way. We all have a spiritual ego, and we can all be taken in by its convincingly sheep-like appearance. As long as we're under the influence of an ego mind, it's safe to assume we'll also be susceptible to the ego's spiritual masquerade. Every part of our 3-D existence is ruled by the ego, after all, and the way we experience spirituality is no exception.

For most of us, this is the hardest place to catch the ego at work, because it's so good at pretending to be benevolent and holy. The ego mind is masterful at cloaking itself in the trappings of Spirit. Without real vigilance on our part it can be very hard to tell the difference, which is why extremely sincere people sometimes commit terrible acts in the name of spirituality.

But the reason I bring this up isn't to warn you against starting an inquisition or a cataclysmic holy war. Chances are, that's not your intention. And you're probably not planning to join a charismatic cult and drink the poisoned Kool-Aid anytime soon.

Those are just examples of the spiritual ego at its most extreme. Yet, long before anybody dreams up the kinds of havoc I just mentioned, they've already fallen prey to a much subtler and seemingly benign aspect of egoic spirituality that often goes undetected: The ego's desire to hand down spiritual judgment. We all do it, at least now and then. We can't help it.

When we judge on behalf of Spirit, it doesn't matter how pure our intentions might be; we may even think we're carrying out divine guidance. Yet there's a very good chance we're acting entirely from the ego mind. How can we tell if we're making spiritual judgments based in ego?

Uh, well, they're spiritual *judgments*.

Spirit never judges. Everything is perfect as it is; all mistakes committed within this fantasy world are overlooked equally, and welcomed back by Oneness into Oneness. So a thought that pits anybody against anybody else could never authentically come from Spirit.

Here is a good example of a typical ego-based spiritual thought form: *My religion is holier than your religion.*

Or how about this variation on a theme: *Although we both practice the same teaching, your interpretation of it is faulty. So I think I'll peel off and create a different sect, where only the purest version is practiced.*

Spirit will only help you remember Oneness. It would never promote an agenda that deepens your belief in separation instead. Any thought that causes division of any kind can only come from the ego.

This is yet another common everyday thought form propagated by the spiritual ego: *I'm more enlightened than you are.*

Oh baby, I know that thought form well. When examined closely, its logic is downright laughable. I absolutely know better. And yet I still find myself unable to resist indulging in it from time to time. So you can take it from me: If you ever catch yourself thinking other people are not as enlightened as you are…it's a good indication *you* are not as enlightened as you think you are.

CRASHING THE GATELESS GATE

"The gateless gate" is a classic Zen koan-ish kind of phrase. A paradoxical statement meant to be pondered as a vehicle for awakening. To me, the gateless gate is something slightly different: A metaphor for the vaporous, mirage-like barrier currently separating our unenlightened awareness from ultimate truth.

This locked gate appears solid and impenetrable until we manage to walk right through it; only then (after our bodies pass effortlessly through this seeming obstruction) does it disappear. And, newly enlightened, we look back at what we thought was a gate, and realize there never was a barrier of any kind. We were mistaken.

Enlightened people often say things like: *Enlightenment is simple! Spiritual seekers put so much effort into trying to awaken, yet no effort is necessary.*

They talk this way because they're trying to tell us accurately and honestly about their own experience. All they did was walk through an open gate, after all. And, as it turns out, they didn't even do that. The gate itself was a figment of their imagination.

Yes. Well. *No effort is necessary* is a great observation. But I've already tried not trying, and that hasn't worked out so well.

Making it through that metaphorical gate is my one ambition—yet in order to pass through it, my mind will have to be strong enough to perceive this impenetrable barrier as the illusory fantasy it really is. Even though it still looks and feels like a solid gate.

To stop being fooled by the seeming reality of the barrier, I'll have to employ non-judgment. I'll have to stop telling myself stories about how solid bodies can't pass through locked gates.

The illusory nature of the gate becomes obvious only *after* you've already seen through the illusion. The gate dissolves, in other words, because by walking through it, you've already proven to yourself it doesn't exist.

•   •   •

Periodically I gather myself and run against the gate in the hope it will reveal its permeability as I get there. I know the locked gate isn't real. I realize my *belief* in the gate is all that keeps me stranded on this side of it. Yet some deeply held part of my mind still firmly accepts the gate's solidity, so I bang up my knees and nose each time I smack into its seemingly impenetrable face. I can't help it: I still judge and resist that gate. On some level I still believe its story.

I look forward to being one of those people who looks back at the gateless gate from my enlightened vantage point, and sees, in retrospect, how foolish I was to work so hard.

Yet for now, I'll keep on working hard to strengthen my own mind. With Spirit's help I'll go on dismantling belief, bit by bit, as I prepare for my next run at the gate.

While that barrier still appears solid as steel, what other option do I have?

CHAPTER NINE

enemy mine

THE PROJECTOR, THE PROJECTION
AND BRITISH PETROLEUM

We (awesome, loose-cannon creators that we are) create everything in our 3-D world, and we sustain these creations with our ongoing belief in them. We don't want to remember we're doing that, and we sure as hell don't want to take responsibility for it.

Since we're so determined to deny that our miscreations come from us, our solution is to project them outward. By pushing them onto the outside world, it means they appear to be happening independently, completely outside of us. This gives us the satisfying illusion that everything is somebody else's fault. And as a result, we get to believe in our own innocence, while we point the finger outside and make others guilty instead of us. And the ego mind loves to facilitate this, because projection reinforces our belief in separation. All of which guarantees we'll stay lost in dreams a whole lot longer. It's a win-win, really.

But we're all about healing our separated minds, you and me. And to do that, we have to retrace our steps. We need to reclaim and reincorporate every single rejected bit of ourselves. Everything that has been projected outward must first be perceived with corrected vision, and then gently welcomed back into the fold. These unacknowledged, "outlaw" portions of our minds are then free to take their rightful places as integral parts of the One healed self.

• • •

I was chatting with my hairdresser, Claudia, awhile back. After we caught up on all our news, she paused and asked if I could help her with a spiritual question that had been troubling her.

"I'm heartsick about the BP oil spill, and all the damage it's caused," she began. "And I want to help. I've been told I should visualize a clean, healed Gulf, and they say if enough of us do that it'll become a reality. But I'm having trouble with that idea; the scale of the disaster seems too huge and overwhelming," she said, adding, "I guess my problem is I don't really believe I'm powerful enough to cause that kind of change."

The BP oil spill had been going on for roughly six weeks at this point. (If you've been living in some other galaxy and didn't hear about this epic environmental catastrophe, I will sum it up quickly for you: In 2010, the Gulf Coast of the United States, still staggering from the devastation wrought in 2005 by Hurricane Katrina, was home to a three-month oil spill courtesy of British Petroleum.)

Anyway, Claudia's question was a good one. How do you pray for change when you don't believe in the power of your own prayer? (Answer: You're pretty much screwed.)

Stated another way, how do you get past the propaganda whispered by your own ego mind—remember, it's only too happy to remind you you're small and powerless—if you're not already in the habit of looking beyond the false images the ego shows you? Same answer: You probably can't.

I told her my approach was different. "I don't give the oil spill any reality," I said. "I don't take it at face value, because I know it's all part of this 3-D illusion. But that doesn't mean I don't take it seriously. If it's playing on my movie screen—and by that, I mean if I'm witnessing it going on in my world—

I know I *must* be running that film in my projector. Everything "out there" is a part of me, so that means it's impossible for the oil spill, or anything else, to come from anyplace outside me."

"Nothing can exist independently of me," I continued. "I'm doing it all by myself, *to* myself. I'm projecting my own unconscious ego crap onto the outside world, so I can make it the bad guy instead of me. But I know perfectly well the oil spill can't originate outside me. The 3-D world is made by me, out of the raw material of me.

That means you, me, and the oil spill are all One. Not in abstract theory, but in actual reality. We are everywhere and everything; there's nothing separate from us.

So I choose to take complete responsibility for what I see out there in the world. I'm doing my best to own all those hateful, unconscious parts of myself. And that includes the oil spill. I'm working to welcome the oil spill back as a "not-guilty" part of my One healed self. I'm pretty sure this is the only kind of healing that will ever make a meaningful difference in the world, no matter how much oil does or doesn't get dumped into the Gulf."

•   •   •

I don't watch the news much anymore. Controversy is king, in the land of the twenty-four-hour news cycle, and I no longer see the point in becoming outraged on purpose. I know it isn't true that anybody "out there" is doing bad things—yet it's still a lot of work, sometimes, to remind myself of that.

If I do happen to catch a news story, I try to hand it over to Spirit right away for reinterpretation. I want to perceive it properly with the kind of purity of vision that I'm rarely capable of, left to my own devices. So I was keeping half an eye on the BP story as it unfolded. And as more and more ugly facts were revealed, I took each one of them and, with Spirit's help, used it as the basis for yet another kind of vision correction exercise.

The first time Spirit suggested this next form of exercise, it was really more of an out-of-body vision-ish thing, with me just observing the symbols that were shown to me. But I've performed the exercise many times since on my own, and I can report there's a lot of power in it. You might find it useful too.

JOINING WITH THE FILMSTRIP

This is how that first exercise unfolded: I began by turning my gaze away from the movie screen, away from the oil-soaked crimes the world was showing me. I faced myself instead and looked deeply inward, until I located the source of these terrible images: The movie projector at the core of my unconscious belief system. And as I closely examined this projector, I recognized firsthand that the contents of the filmstrip were actually the same as what I was seeing projected on the outside.

I moved in closer, until I merged and became One with the contents of the filmstrip. I allowed the circumstances of the oil spill to just be. I owned the oil spill; the dead wildlife; the corrupt or inept officials. The victims were me, the perpetrators were me, the bystanders were me. I acknowledged and accepted them all, staying within that joined awareness until I authentically experienced them as parts of myself. Until I felt our mutual Oneness in my stomach.

And here's the interesting thing: As I felt our mutual Oneness, I was automatically flooded with tenderness for these exiled parts of myself. Because in that moment, I knew for certain that everything *except* the Oneness was just a bunch of made-up stories. Meaningless shadows flickering on my movie screen, and nothing more.

I felt completely at peace with the oil spill. Oneness is only possible through non-judgment, and non-judgment means everything merely *is*. And it's all good, exactly as it is. No judgment of the BP situation was possible, once all parts were genuinely accepted and welcomed home into Oneness.

Jesus rather famously said, "Love your enemies." Which, Eckhart Tolle points out, is really the same thing as saying, "*Have* no enemies."

The madness of the world originates in our split-off fantasies of denial and projection—nowhere else. It's only in madness that enemies can exist. Replace judgment and projection with acceptance and Oneness, and the opposite of madness immediately reveals itself. And with sanity, love emerges and belief in enemies is no longer possible.

And now we come back to the question of "doing something to help." Am I saying it's wrong to donate money, or go wash seabirds, or lobby for tighter legislation? Or even, if you feel so inclined, to visualize a sparkly clean Gulf Coast?

Of course not. Like I said before, you should do as you feel you must, to ease the pain of 3-D dreaming.

Just understand that's not where the real work lies.

Whenever I catch myself getting outraged at what's playing on my movie screen, I stop. I know it's a perfect opportunity for vision correction. My ego mind is always hard at work manufacturing those dark, unconscious filmstrips of judgment and condemnation. I welcome the chance to correct my mistaken perceptions wherever I can.

It seems to me, if I keep working until the contents of the filmstrip become so perfectly purified they reflect the light of ultimate truth and nothing else...sooner or later there'll be no more need for the projector itself.

Without a projector, there's no separate perception. And with unified perception, true Oneness can't be far behind.

Or so it seems to me.

· · ·

Before we move on, I want to talk a bit more about the principle at the heart of the previous exercise, because it's so important. Until you experience it for yourself, it may seem hard to imagine that judgment and condemnation could evaporate into nothing when "the enemy" is accepted in Oneness. Yet I'm fairly certain this is the foundation of truth on which all awakening rests.

I've experienced this surprising process more than once; although I didn't realize it at the time, the final episode in *Long Time No See** contained what would be my first of many tastes of this same powerful lesson.

But something happened last winter to show me more about the meaning of this lesson. I blogged about it at the time, but I want to recount some of the events here in more detail:

Last week I had the house to myself; my husband was in Japan for his annual Buddhist pilgrimage.

For several weeks prior to his trip we'd been noticing an unusual buildup in the ant population surrounding our house. Columns and battalions, wave after wave of ant reinforcements marching in busy streams all around our property. Kurt commented on more than one occasion that the first rainfall would surely bring a huge infestation into our kitchen.

And it did exactly that, the day after he left for Japan. Ants on the countertops, ants climbing the walls, cavorting in the cupboards, exploring the trashcan, carrying off the bowl of cat food. (Well, maybe not that last one. But nearly.)

And at first I went to that place of "us versus them," trying to kill them all and make sure they didn't come back.

---

*It's a two-parter entitled *Who eats what?* In it, a great blue heron and a work-related adversary share top billing as the enemy *du jour.*

I cleaned the cupboards and countertops, I took out the trash, I drowned as many ants as I could find. And in spite of my efforts, the infestation doubled in size over the next few hours.

Then I caught myself and realized what I was doing. Of my many conversations with Spirit, a significant number of them have dealt with this very subject of "us versus them." That there's no such thing as "them," and no such thing as someone or something outside oneself to be protected from.

So I looked down at the moving streams of ants and thought, Ok, I'll find the connection of Oneness that I share with you, and I'll use it for communication purposes. When I can feel our joined awareness, I'll tell you to leave my house, and that you should save yourselves by going away peacefully. Because I really don't want to have to kill all of you.

(As any student of Oneness knows, that's a compromise use of Oneness that I was planning to try. In connecting with the eternal Oneness of those ants, I was intending to overlook the 3-D reality of their ant-selves, but not overlook the 3-D reality of my kitchen. A flawed strategy to be sure, but I figured it was better than wholesale ant murder, which was my Plan B.)

As I closed my eyes to begin joining with those ants in Oneness, a remarkable thing happened. I felt them as thousands of individual sparks of my own divine self; saw them as thousands of points of perfect radiant light. And a tremendous sense of gratitude and tender affection unexpectedly welled up in me. I loved those thousands of little pieces of myself, and I wanted to know them better. It seemed the most natural thing in the world to merge gently into One shared awareness.

Part of me was still thinking: Ok, you've connected with the ants, now tell them to get out of your kitchen. *But to my surprise I found I didn't care about my kitchen anymore. In fact, I couldn't have cared about my kitchen if I tried. Once you've managed to choose Oneness—and it's such a good feeling, there's no motivation to switch allegiance and choose anything else instead—all 3-D concerns completely lose their meaning. You'd have to willingly turn your back on the Oneness to be able to care about any part of this illusory world.*

The feeling of Oneness is so suffused with radiant truth, its divine light blots out all 3-D illusion the way sunshine melts darkness. Where does the darkness go after the sun kisses the horizon and lights up the sky? Who cares? After it happens, the only thing that matters is the glorious dawn.

I couldn't care about my kitchen, because the kitchen wasn't real—the divine perfection of those ants was my only reality. So I offered them my love, my reverence and my gratitude for the remainder of that meditation. And I knew when I opened my eyes and went to check the kitchen, the ants would be gone.

And they were.

At the time, I was mostly just tickled I'd found a non-toxic way to make the ants go away. But really, I didn't "make" the ants do anything. My One self, in its great love for me, gathered together a few thousand bits of myself to teach me a beautiful lesson: The inextricable link between non-judgment—the inability to make up stories about the state of my kitchen—and Oneness.

I wasn't able to find the ants guilty of trespassing, and as a result of our shared connection they wordlessly understood my 3-D dilemma and willingly chose to go back outside, and find some other place to take shelter from the rain.

Does Oneness always result in happy 3-D endings like that one? Um, probably not.

Yet in my own limited experience, I am treated so gently and lovingly by my unseen Teacher that the answer tends to be yes. I learn my lessons of Oneness and my 3-D problems are gently resolved at the same time. But once again, your results may vary.

Either way, the beauty and importance of the lesson remains the same. Any worldly problem-solving that may tag along behind it is just icing on the cake.

Really, all this is just another way of circling back to that question asked by *A Course in Miracles*: Do you want to be right or happy? Do you want to experience the profound joy of Oneness firsthand, or do you prefer fantasy judgment instead?

Happy is the end of right; right is the end of happy. It's your choice to make—but you definitely can't have both.

IN THE WORLD? OR OF THE WORLD? – PART III
ON BATTLING ILLNESS

Over the years I've had pretty good success with the spontaneous healing of minor illnesses, especially cold and flu. I found if I simply refused to be sick, the virus or bacteria would lose power and immediately melt away.

A handy skill, to be sure. Yet, underlying the refusal to be sick was the assumption that these microbes were an "us versus them" enemy to be conquered. And I find I don't want to make enemies, anymore.

Just because I don't want to make an enemy of illness, however, doesn't mean I welcome it either. (Maybe a master of non-judgment would find illness and non-illness equally acceptable. I ain't there yet.)

When I feel a cold or flu coming on, these are the steps I take nowadays: First I put out the clear intention that I choose health. Through self-inquiry, I make sure I'm not harboring any secret desire to abdicate responsibility and go to bed for a few days.

Next, in a combined film reel/joining pool meditation, I focus inward until I can feel the radiant pinprick light of innocence within each of those microbes. And just like the kitchen example with the ants, feeling this light within each microbe causes me to spontaneously feel love and gratitude for them. I recognize these former outlaw enemies as microscopic bits of my divine self. And finally, together with these divine micro-bits, I leap into the joining pool and stay there with them for as long as I can manage it.

Although we're only discussing minor illness here, I suspect this practice would be valuable no matter what the physical ailment might be. I've only been practicing this for a short time, but so far I've found it seems to work fairly well at dissolving illusory 3-D sickness.

What it's doing to heal my *real* sickness, on the other hand, is immeasurable.

SELF-INQUIRY – PART II

In the beginning of this book I described the kinds of questions you'd want to ask yourself about every aspect of your 3-D existence: *Is this true? Do I really know it's true, or is this merely an assumption I've always accepted at face value? What do I know for certain?*

Fans of Byron Katie's *The Work*™ will no doubt recognize a similarity to the four questions she uses in her process of inquiry: *Is it true? Can you absolutely know it's true? How do you react when you believe that thought? Who would you be without the thought?*

This is likely no accident. Although Katie herself doesn't typically use words like enlightenment or self-realization to describe her own state of awareness, it's pretty clear from listening to her speak that she is no longer fooled by the 3-D stories the world presents to her. She seems to have awakened permanently into a state in which she is free of the resistance usually manufactured by the ego mind. She has become, in her words, "a lover of what is."

She says self-inquiry is the tool she used to achieve this radical change in perception. However, she doesn't teach self-inquiry to the rest of us with the insistence that it be used as a blowtorch-covered wrecking ball (even though there's a fair possibility that is how she originally used it herself).

Although she recommends we use her system of inquiry in every aspect of our lives, she also offers it as a more targeted tool. Even if we're not yet interested in total demolition, we can still use her system whenever we find ourselves suffering because we believe a stressful or painful thought is true. So, in the hands of this uncommonly practical and compassionate teacher, self-inquiry often becomes a razor-sharp implement for lancing a boil or removing a wart. And many people have therefore benefited from these minor surgeries.

I suppose only the tiniest percentage of us will go on to use self-inquiry (whether Byron Katie's four questions, or other ones of our own design) on *every* thought. Lancing a boil is one thing; chopping the entire body to bits is quite another. Yet true freedom lies in the willingness to sign up for the chopping.

SELF-INQUIRY COMBINED WITH JOINING POOL MEDITATION

Self-inquiry is all about getting to the root of false thoughts and beliefs we hold about ourselves and our world. Once we see what these thoughts are made of, we can then work to be free of them. There are a number of ways to dig down and isolate these false beliefs; this is one I particularly like.

If I notice I'm harboring a gut anxiety or any form of mental disquiet, I try to stop what I'm doing and perform this exercise. I still begin with the cavern and the pool, but instead of leaving my baggage on the bank before jumping into the water, I do something a bit different. I turn and squarely face the unpleasant thought or belief that's causing my disquiet. I let all mental thoughts about the problem slip away, until I'm left only with the *feeling* the thought or belief produces. Then I bring the feeling with me as I slip into the water.

After I've dissolved my body and mind and have become One with Source to the best of my ability, I focus all my awareness on that feeling I brought with me. I don't think about it, I just stay present with the feeling until it unfolds and shows me what it's really made of. (It will likely be made of fear, hate, guilt, shame or some combination of these.) When I've seen clearly what the feeling is made of, I just offer it acceptance.

It's important not to analyze it or think about it in any way. No judgment, no stories about it, no sense of right or wrong. I just feel it, accept it and allow it to dissolve into One.

This is a more powerful practice than it may seem at first glance. Even though it is accomplished with gentleness and without analysis, I've found it to be very effective at undoing false thoughts and beliefs.

This gentle process on its own may not be enough for the stickiest, most persistent beliefs buried in your unconscious mind. If you've tried to free yourself from a persistent belief using the above exercise a few dozen times to no avail, a more direct form of self-inquiry may be needed.

You'll want to turn and face that unpleasant or scary belief, and look at it unflinchingly. Examine it carefully and honestly from every angle. Dig until you've reached its very core. *Feel the intense discomfort this thought or belief produces, as fully as you can.* While you're feeling that pain or fear, ask yourself all the appropriate self-inquiry questions to determine whether you're sure it's true. Don't stop questioning it until you're absolutely certain of the answer. And when you authentically realize the thought or belief isn't true, focus only on that painful feeling, and offer it compassion. Thank it for having done such a fine job of carrying out your mistaken wishes for so long. And then release it, allowing it to dissolve.

•   •   •

I should probably mention that none of the exercises in this book are likely to be a constant, ongoing thing. Well, they're not an ongoing thing for me, anyway. I get inspired to start one form of exercise and I do it for a few days or a few weeks, before life invariably intervenes and presents me with new challenges or new inspirations.

I might do a few days of concentrated self-inquiry, followed by two weeks of forgiveness, followed by five days where I find it next to impossible to quiet my mind or focus enough to accomplish anything at all. This is an up-and-down process, at least in my experience; although the overall movement is always toward strength and sanity and peace, none of it ever seems to be achieved in an orderly linear fashion. But who knows—your experience with it might be different.

If your process is similar to mine, however, try not to sweat it too much. Don't beat yourself up if you can't sustain any one form of vision correction for long. Keep it fluid, change it up as you see fit, and revisit an exercise whenever you feel inspired to do so. Inspiration is a key ingredient in this sort of work; there's little point in just going through the motions here. Sincerity is everything.

THE DEVIL YOU KNOW

Here's something else to consider as you're turning around to squarely face your scary or painful belief: Are you absolutely sure you want to let it go?

We humans are a strange bunch. Given the choice between familiar pain and unfamiliar healing, we tend to choose the pain every time. We've built many of our most deeply ingrained personal stories around pain management. We're accustomed to living with pain; it defines who we think we are. We're not so sure we want to rock the boat by choosing healing, which would then force us to rearrange our stories in unknown ways.

This means we might get into an exercise like the one we just talked about, and find ourselves suddenly stalled at the most important point. We felt the fear and pain, we asked all the right self-inquiry questions to determine the belief wasn't true. We thanked it sincerely. And then…nothing. Because we just can't seem to let it go. Could it be this painful belief is still here because it serves our ego's needs in some way?

This is where another couple of self-inquiry questions may be helpful.

Am I really ready to release this pain?
If not, why not?
The answers may surprise you.

CHAPTER TEN

other
supplemental practices

I've found the following disciplines are extremely useful for strengthening and retraining the mind. Together they fall under the general heading of mind mastery.

In my experience, none of these practices lead directly to awakening; observing the mind alone probably won't get you there. A practice of being present likely won't do it either. Meditation by itself is wonderful, but it may not be enough.

The point of all these very worthy practices is to put your mind on a fitness program, so you'll be better equipped when the moment comes, to choose between permanent awakening and falling back to sleep.

MIND MASTERY

Left to its own devices, the thinking mind is like an unsupervised eight-year-old. It runs around the house all day in its Batman cape, yelling at the top of its lungs just because it can. Its diet consists of marshmallows and soda pop. Hasn't brushed its teeth or washed behind its ears in years. All this freedom isn't making your eight-year-old mind happy, by the way; it's just very accustomed to getting its own way.

If you're a responsible adult, you may not recognize this undisciplined description of your own mind at first glance. After all, you hold a job/raise a family/attend college or possibly all of the above and more. That requires dedication and discipline. Right?

We're talking about a different kind of discipline, here. When I first attempted any of the following exercises, I was surprised to discover how lax my mind really is. In trying for the first time to exercise this sort of control over mental function, it quickly becomes obvious just how unfamiliar and difficult a job it is to set and enforce boundaries for that strong-willed, bratty little junk food addict.

OBSERVING THE MIND

On paper, observing the mind sounds simple: Just step back and notice your own thoughts from time to time throughout the day. Easy, right?

Go ahead and try it; see how your sugar-fueled eight-year-old likes the sudden adult supervision. If your mind is anything like mine, this simple practice won't be so easy.

Yet observing your own thoughts is key to so many aspects of vision correction. It's the primary tool for discerning whether you're mistaking ego for Spirit, for example. If you're not noticing spiritual judgments as they occur, how can you hope to recognize the deception?

Being able to tell Spirit from ego requires vigilance, and another name for vigilance is observing your own mind. Notice your thoughts, and pause to see what they're made of. Do they promote unity and non-judgment? They're probably Spirit-inspired. Do they promote anything else? Well, nothing besides Oneness is true—and guess who's in charge of everything that isn't truth?

When it comes down to it, mind observation is useful for almost every kind of vision correction. By noticing the contents of our minds throughout the day, it makes us that much more likely to be aware of judgmental thoughts as they creep in.

And by judgmental, I mean any mistaken thought that strengthens the idea of separation. These thoughts hurt us, because they aren't true. If you're paying attention to your own judgmental thoughts, you'll start to feel them as the painful lies they really are; you'll notice you feel added mental stress and/or physical discomfort.

To be in the habit of noticing mistaken thoughts as they occur gives us the opportunity to perform proactive vision correction. Like I said before, it's just an opportunity. It might still be a struggle to want to see beyond the ego's interpretation of things, but you've gotta start somewhere, right?

At least we're aware now that something isn't being seen properly, and we recognize we're feeling discomfort because of it. The goal, of course, is to override egoic resistance as soon as we notice it. But even if we don't always choose to undo it right away, we can make a mental note to perform a little vision correction work later on.

．　　．　　．

Another interesting phenomenon might occur as you begin to notice the thoughts that flit though your conscious mind; you might start catching some of the nasty lies your ego whispers below the surface, too.

Not the really deep unconscious stuff—just some of the cruelly nonsensical crap your ego mind feeds you every day. Now, instead of swallowing it unchallenged, you can notice it, look at what it's made of and choose whether or not to believe any of it.

I've learned a lot about myself since I began observing the contents of my own mind. As it turns out, my ego has been quite busy in the propaganda department. For instance, I found out I didn't like or trust myself, especially when it came to public speaking.

I knew much of my fear of public speaking stemmed from having to let people look at me; even after all these years I was still deeply uncomfortable in my own skin. Yet I had no idea I was also carrying an abiding grudge against my own mental processes.

It seemed I hated my own untrustworthy and unpredictable brain. I was afraid the moment I stepped in front of a group, my mind would wander all over the place and I'd ramble pointlessly like somebody's senile auntie. Or maybe I'd suddenly blank out and stare helplessly at the crowd until it was time for us all to go home, a victim of my own socially inept geekitude.

At heart, I realized I was afraid I would bore everyone. As my ego mind gleefully reminded me, I was a dull, drippy nerd who would surely put listeners to sleep. And I had to admit the ego's arguments were persuasive; years ago, whenever I opened my mouth to talk, people used to show visible annoyance at the thought of having to listen to me. They'd often get up and leave the room, or interrupt and start conversations on another topic.

I realized they were mirroring my own belief in my unworthiness. I didn't think I had anything worthwhile to say, so why should they? With the help of my Buddhist practice I explored this core belief I held about myself. After a decade or so of determined work, I began to authentically feel I was worthy of being listened to. And as I healed this misperception about my own value, the dismissive reactions from listeners gradually faded and disappeared.

Not only did the dismissive reactions disappear, I began to get the opposite response; in recent years, people often seemed to hang on my every word. And it had been at least a decade since anyone had cut me off or left the room. I'd forgotten I ever used to worry about such things.

I was still plenty apprehensive at the thought of speaking publicly, but I had always assumed it was because I was shy. Afraid of strangers. More comfortable in the shadows. It wasn't until I really stopped to take a look at my own unexamined thoughts that I realized how much abuse and mistrust I still regularly heaped on my own mental processes.

You can't heal what you don't know about, right?

Now, thanks to observation of my thoughts, I had the opportunity to do forgiveness work, and as much self-inquiry as necessary to get to the root of this mistaken and unloving attitude I still held toward myself.

This is just one example of why I say mind observation is an irreplaceable partner in this vision correction process. If you're preparing to hit the (metaphorical) road in search of enlightenment, my advice is: Don't leave home without it.

NO-MIND MEDITATION

No-mind meditation is what people are usually referring to when they talk about meditation. It's exactly what it sounds like: The idea is to experience yourself without the intrusive presence of your own thoughts. It takes practice and discipline to be able to quiet the jabbering of the ego mind, leaving only stillness in its wake. Yet cultivation of stillness is indispensable to any serious practice of Oneness.

I'm relatively new to the practice of no-mind meditation; in Nichiren Buddhism, the chanting of Nam Myoho Renge Kyo is performed with eyes open and an active mind. At first I found it rather difficult to unlearn those habits of practice and embrace the no-mind opposite. Because I found it so hard to make my mind shut up, I was never particularly drawn to meditation as a practice. And as long as I only made half-hearted attempts to practice meditation, I remained not very good at it.

Funny how that works.

It was only after I began to spend quality time in the joining pool, that the practice of no-mind meditation came alive for me. There I was, disintegrating happily in the Source-water; yet I discovered once the body parts dissolved and the thinking mind dissolved, the joining with Spirit could only be accomplished in stillness. And once accomplished, it could only be sustained in *prolonged* stillness. The kind of stillness that doesn't come without practice.

Suddenly a supplemental discipline of no-mind meditation seemed like an incredibly good idea. And it is. I heartily recommend it.

BEING IN THE NOW

The eternal truth of Oneness can only be experienced in the now. Past and future are ego inventions designed to keep us preoccupied with things that don't exist, thus keeping our attention focused away from the now. If you need proof, just try hanging out in the present moment and see how long it takes your ego mind to change the subject. As I said before, one of the ways to describe the ego mind is *resistance to what is*. And *what is* can only be experienced in the now.

Much is made of the practice of being in the now. And I'm not saying that like it's a bad thing. Meditation, contemplation—anything that brings you into the state of present moment awareness is a great practice. It's wonderful to discover how luminous, how beautifully alive the world seems when viewed in the now. Present moment awareness strengthens and disciplines the mind; it also helps teach us what the world looks like without ego interpretation.

The now is a very powerful place to be.

Yet as long as we're voluntarily ruled by an ego mind, practicing awareness of the now by itself probably won't be enough to lead directly to enlightenment. The ego mind is not likely to allow it.

Don't forget, you're still playing games inside the ego's casino; it holds all the winning cards. So if your practice of the now moment gets too strong for the ego's liking, it'll just arrange worldly events to distract your thinking mind to focus on past or future fantasy instead. And you probably won't have much say in the matter.

The permanent now is a hallmark of a person who has already

awakened. It's a side effect of enlightenment, in other words, as opposed to a catalyst for it. Trying to stay fully in the now before you've self-realized is kind of like trying to extinguish all desire before you've self-realized. Ego minds are all about desire—they endlessly want something, anything, other than what is.

Trying to get to enlightenment by extinguishing desire is a hopeless quest. Although relinquishment of desire is a noble and helpful form of exercise, it can never fully succeed as long as the ego mind is in charge. Desire will disappear on its own when the ego mind is discarded, not before.

Likewise, the permanent now is a part of the truth that is blocked by the ego. When the ego goes, the now is revealed in its absence.

Having said all that, practice of the now does play a vital role in vision correction. That's because the goal is to be able to stay fully aware so we can practice vision correction in real-time.

When we experience something that makes us believe in ego fantasy, that belief hurts; it disrupts our peace. To recognize this descent into fantasy and gently correct the misperception almost as quickly as it happens, requires—among other things—a damn strong practice of present moment awareness.

It's a goal we're not likely to attain one hundred percent of the time, at least not without some degree of permanent awakening under our belts. Yet it's still a practice well worth striving for.

NON-RESISTANCE

Non-resistance always seemed like a very straightforward concept at first glance; something that needed no further explanation. And I would try to practice it from time to time, usually when I had no other choice.

Like when stuck in gridlocked traffic, or left standing for an hour on concrete in high heels. After the first flash of irritation I would usually try practicing non-resistance to what is. Because it's obvious that even in 3-D, it's not the traffic or the inappropriate footwear that are causing my suffering—it's my reaction to them.

Yet let's not forget the egoic description we've spoken of throughout this book: The ego mind *itself* is resistance to what is. So non-resistance isn't really just an idle pastime to play with when things aren't going my way (although there's nothing wrong with that). It's a tool for helping undo the ego mind itself. And when combined with self-inquiry, the dismantling power of non-resistance knows no limits.

Since I've begun walking the path of the Serious Beginner, I've been using non-resistance to explore previously forbidden territory deep within my own ego mind. You know the areas I mean—those fear places, the ones we usually try our best not to visit. We all have them. We know they're there, but we put up walls to block them from view; we play loud music to drown the sound of our own worried whispers.

It might be the fear that a child or spouse will die before we do. Or fear of financial insolvency and homelessness. Or the fear that our bodies will unexpectedly betray us, manufacturing cancer or some other horrifying disease.

This fear is muffled, of course, by the walls we've built, and the loud music we play to drown the ego's dark mutterings.

Recently, I got sick of it. Sick of the walls, sick of the energy I spend avoiding fear. And that's a good thing. I've halfheartedly tried to perform forgiveness work on my "dark matter" in the past, because I know intellectually it's all an illusion. But my ego mind and I always jointly agreed this particular stuff was too deep and uncomfortable, and far too powerful for me to tackle right now. Better to leave it for later.

But then one night, later became now. It was not so much the dark matter itself, but my frightened resistance to it that was suddenly unacceptable. I clearly saw my own sick role in upholding the drama, and I didn't want to do it anymore. And as soon as I decided to stop participating in the fear, Spirit stepped in and guided me in meditation.

Much like the "bits and pieces" vision I told you about earlier, I was both inside and outside this experience at the same time. So I got to feel it firsthand, and also observe it as an impartial bystander. This is what I saw:

I was shown that we build walls against our fears, but the walls themselves are not solid. They're made out of resistance. I was given to understand that we build these walls of resistance because our ego mind assures us they will protect us from our fears. But ego minds lie—so the opposite is actually true.

On closer examination, I saw my wall of resistance was made up of an energy field. This field served two purposes. By staying clenched in permanent spasm, it created and sustained the illusion of a solid wall (much like the energy spasms that created fake gaps between individual shards in the earlier vision of separated bits and pieces). Its second purpose was even more critical: The constant supply of energy delivered by this permanent spasm was actually the food source that fueled the fear and kept it alive.

In other words, without the energy of resistance, there's nothing to sustain fear. The two go hand in hand. Stop resisting a fearful thought, then, and that thought is bound to lose its emotional charge. Let the wall crumble, and the fear soon follows suit.

Armed with this new insight about fear and non-resistance, I've been going deep into unconscious ego territory whenever I can. I want to dismantle these big, bad, scary belief systems by putting an end to resistance.

I ask for help in this, of course. I join with Spirit before I embark on these archaeological digs. And then in my meditations I squarely face the fear and allow all possible consequences of that fear into my mind. I invite it to do its worst—not in a defiant way, but with complete non-resistance to it. All outcomes are equally ok, because all are equally unreal. All are part of the same dream.

I hold this non-resistant invitation in my mind until the energy spasm of fear and denial begins to dissolve. I watch as the wall loses power and fades away. Then I flood that previously resistant "wall" space with simple awareness. And then, finally, with acceptance.

Try it for yourself, if it interests you. Next time you're caught up in a deeply fearful thought, stop what you're doing. Take time to go within and be with Spirit. Get centered. When you feel like you're ready, ask Spirit to go with you to examine this fearful thought together.

Notice your resistance to the fearful thought. Ask Spirit to help you stop resisting it. Whatever it is you're afraid of, just let the fearful thought flow over you and through you, and don't fight back. Let it flow, and keep on flowing.

And then notice what happens to the fearful thought.

I've found that just the action of turning to face the ick—of agreeing to end my participation in a deeply held fear fantasy—tends to cause major shifts in the state of things.

And this is the true power of non-resistance. If self-inquiry is the flaming torch that lights up the darkness, non-resistance sucks all the juice out of the scary monsters revealed in that torchlight. And (much the same way enemies stop being enemies once you've perceived them properly), I find monsters aren't really monsters anymore, when you've stopped being scared of them and accepted them as they are.

CHAPTER ELEVEN

manifestation
and oneness

THE ATTRACTIVE LAW OF ATTRACTION

One might not expect to find a section on Law of Attraction teachings in a book about Oneness; after all, manifestation teachings seem, at first glance, to be in opposition to teachings of Oneness.

The Law of Attraction (let's shorten it to LOA) is usually understood as being all about attracting good stuff into our 3-D existence. And if we've identified an area of lack in our lives and wish to remedy it through LOA, that means we believe the ego's version of the story. We're making the good and bad of this world real. And that's not Oneness.

Yet I've always had a soft spot for manifestation teachings. Yes, in their "getting good stuff" form, they function purely as expedient means teachings. They don't point directly to the truth. But like all good expedient means teachings, LOA reaches people where they're at right now, engaging them at their current level of spiritual understanding and current level of need. And at the same time as it delivers on its promise of relieving worldly suffering, it subtly hints at deeper truths that can help the student grow in awareness.

However, LOA is also much more than a vehicle for getting stuff. When understood in a broader context, it becomes an important vision correction tool. And that is a teaching that *does* point to Oneness.

Yet even in its classic "getting good stuff" form, LOA teaches us to begin shedding the victim identity of the ego mind, as we gradually open ourselves to the possibility of our own unfathomable power. It's only a small piece of the Oneness puzzle, but the authentic realization that we are not at the mercy of random outside forces can be a profound doorway into ultimate truth.

•   •   •

Before we get into a serious discussion of the benefits of LOA in a practice of Oneness (and yes, there are some astonishingly powerful benefits), maybe we should back up and go over the basics of manifestation. Just to make sure we're all on the same page.

The following is a brief primer on classic LOA manifestation, as it pertains to our larger topic of Oneness. It explains both the basic steps involved and the underlying mechanics of the law, along with their place in the overall Oneness scheme of things.

In this section, I use examples that make it seem as if our principle concern is to rearrange the details of our 3-D dream world. I do this because that's the easiest way of explaining the basics of how and why the law of 3-D causation (also known as LOA) works. Please keep in mind we'll be discussing the deeper significance of LOA afterward.

LAW OF ATTRACTION BASICS

As we have learned, the world is caused by mental activity. Our mental activity. Yours and mine. The world is also made of mental activity. Everything within the world is both caused by, and made of, our own thoughts, beliefs and feelings.

In other words, nothing in 3-D is beyond our control. Nothing happens *to* us. Nothing is caused by outside forces. The way each of us experiences our world is the direct result of our own individual feelings about the world. When we learn to guide our own inner feelings about the world, we reinvent the circumstances of our outer world as well.

You yourself can begin to exercise control over the shifting details of your 3-D dream world, first by realizing what the world is actually made of, and then by actively choosing what you want to have in it. *Because mental activity is the one-and-only source of power here within the dream.* Mental activity is the cause, and the 3-D world is the effect.

Let's say you're walking around in your everyday 3-D reality, and there's something about your personal circumstance you wish could be better. What you're experiencing right now in your world is the effect of your own previous mental activity. (And for larger aspects of your world, like pollution or economic crises, you're experiencing the effects of previous *collective* mental activity. But let's focus on your own unique circumstances—your own health, relationships, wealth or general happiness. Less complicated.)

"Oh, no sweat," you say. "You tell me I can affect my environment through my own mental activity, so I'll just think positive thoughts and wish for better stuff from now on. Then my world will be just like I want it to be."

Not so fast.

As we talked about earlier in this book, most of our mental activity is not performed consciously. Our unconscious minds are doing most of the heavy lifting, whether we're asleep or awake.

And as we well know, the unconscious part of the ego mind is not a happy thinker. The unconscious is where our darkest, most irrational doubts and fears reside. The unconscious ego mind is working industriously, twenty-four/seven, spewing out its worries and pet peeves onto the 3-D world. And the 3-D world—being only a mirror, a shadow, an effect of our mental activity—has no choice but to reflect the reality of this unconscious mental activity back at us.

The 3-D world would not exist if it were not constantly being created and recreated by mental activity. It is entirely dependent on our mental activity for its ongoing "reality." The good news: Because the world is nothing, because it is so pliable and insubstantial on its own, our circumstances can be changed at any moment we choose to take conscious responsibility for our thoughts.

In other words, we manifest all the "realities" and moment-to-moment circumstances in our lives and world, solely through our mental activity. We do this unceasingly, and it happens either consciously or unconsciously. With us, or without us.

FEELING BECOMES FACT

Desires are born as we respond to the circumstances of our 3-D world. *I wish I had that.* Or, *I don't want any more of this.* A desire begins as a thought, yet if it remains a thought alone, it holds no power. Harness that same thought to a feeling, however—a spasm of longing connected to *I wish I had that*, or a quick stab of anger intertwined with *I don't want any more of this*—and suddenly the desire is activated. It becomes a catalyst for causing the very tangible stuff your 3-D dream world is made of.

If we believe something is true and that belief carries an emotional charge with it, the belief is now an activated desire. Our inner creator-self accepts the activated desire without question, and immediately starts to fashion a tangible outer world that conforms with the inner activated belief. The inner creator-self exercises no discrimination in this; it holds no opinions or judgments about our feelings, or our personal worthiness, or our version of the facts. It is entirely neutral.

If you authentically feel something is true, your inner creator-self will automatically begin to create and reflect that "truth" back to you in the form of your outer 3-D experience. This is what we unconscious creators do—even as we emphatically deny our own limitless creative power, we can't help but create constantly, given the required stimulus for 3-D creation.*

---

*Naturally, the stimulus for true creation (the kind of creation you'd perform in the role of a Creator) would be unconditional love. But here inside the casino, any old emotion will do to cause us to go through the motions of creation.

And as in our earlier example of fixed belief in Satanic forces, if you believe in anything firmly enough, no matter what it is, it becomes real for you. And you then experience all the very real, tangible effects associated with that belief. Such is the creative power of activated desire.

Let's look at an example of mundane inner belief, and see how it affects outer reality. Let's say you've never considered yourself a lucky person. Hold a thought like *I never win anything*, and if a sudden pang of despair accompanies the belief, that thought is now an activated desire. So the inner creator-self sees to it that your activated desire becomes your 3-D reality. You'll be left with your losing raffle ticket just as you requested, and somebody else will walk away with the grand prize.

When we don't make conscious efforts to guide all this ongoing mental power, most of what we experience here in our 3-D world tends to be just like the raffle example: More of the same. Past experience of losing raffles causes us to believe we are losers of raffles. The memory of losing combined with the feeling of being a loser causes the perpetuation of the cycle, keeping the circumstances of loss active in our present reality.

Not everyone suffers from raffle envy, of course; for every loser there's someone else who regularly wins at games of chance. But everybody's life contains areas of chronic weakness or sadness or lack. That's the nature of existence in the 3-D dream world. Yet we needn't ever perceive ourselves as helpless victims of forces far greater than ourselves. We can remake our world as we see fit. We can train ourselves to imagine a desired outcome and *feel its reality*, which causes the outer world to conform to the inner belief. By choosing to harness this power, nothing in the world is beyond our scope. Everything becomes possible.

MIND MASTERY – PART II

Yes, that's right—mind mastery plays an important role in LOA teachings, too. To use any manifestation technique effectively, we'll need to exercise some control over those undisciplined minds of ours. (Right now, we're discussing the kind of manifestation training one might receive while learning to become a shaman. You didn't really expect it to be easy, did you?)

As with any form of mind mastery, it begins with simply learning to observe our own thoughts. We tend to spend most of our time on autopilot; this kind of unguided thinking won't cut it if we want to actively shape the ongoing formation of our own reality.

We need to be aware of what our minds are really up to, from moment to moment. Negative thoughts and feelings bring guaranteed negative results, so if we desire more positive outcomes, we need to gain as much insight as possible into our habitual thinking. We don't know what's lurking in our deepest unconscious, of course, but by learning to pay attention to the unexamined thoughts and feelings that flit through our conscious minds, we can begin to sort out the helpful thoughts and discard the ones we don't want.

And no, I'm not talking about denial.

Suppressing bad feelings, papering them over with happy fantasy thoughts—that will get you nowhere in a hurry. Bad, bad shaman. The idea is to become *more* aware of the workings of your own mind, not less. Your job is to develop the discipline, first to uncover the real thoughts lurking in your mind and observe them clearly, then refuse to entertain the negative ones.

Look squarely at those unhelpful thoughts, and then choose not to believe in them. Once that is accomplished, you can learn to replace the negative thoughts with thoughts of the outcome you prefer instead.

Let's say, for example, that someone gives you a tip about a fantastic job opening. You're qualified for it. Getting the job would be a dream come true. *You want that job*, and so a desire is born. And it's an activated desire, because it's accompanied by a great rush of longing. So what's stopping you, then, from being able to make that dream a reality? If your career is an area of weakness in your life, it's because your habitual thoughts and feelings about your livelihood are working against you.

So it's time to take a look at the subtler, unacknowledged thoughts that are sabotaging your activated desire. The thoughts will vary with each individual, of course, but here are some of the likely culprits: *I'm not good enough. I'm a loser and I don't deserve to succeed. I'm a fraud, and if I get the job everyone will know I don't really belong there. I'll just screw it up like I always do.*

Observe those thoughts. It isn't necessary that you try to change your deepest beliefs about yourself. In fact it's a complete waste of time to insist *I'm a winner! I deserve this success*, if, deep down, you truly believe the opposite.

You're only required to recognize that these negative thoughts are merely stories you've been telling yourself. They're just thoughts, and thoughts can be changed. Maybe they've caused you to lose out on good jobs (or winning raffle tickets) in the past, but that doesn't mean you have to perpetuate the same cycle now. Stop allowing those thoughts to slip by unchallenged.

Notice a negative thought, and recognize it as part of an unhelpful thought pattern you've returned to again and again.

Now is your chance to disrupt the cycle. This is where mind mastery plays one of its most beneficial roles.

Ignore the "reality" you've always accepted as the truth of your experience. Do this by refusing to feel the emotions that usually accompany those habitual negative thoughts. *I'm not good enough? Whatever. Maybe it's true and maybe it isn't, but right now I'm just going to allow the thought to come and go without buying into it emotionally.*

Without a feeling attached, the thought immediately loses its creative power. That alone is a huge accomplishment. If you can manage to observe these thoughts that have typically caused you pain in the past, and then make the choice not to allow those same emotions to occur in the present, you will have begun to break up the negative thought patterns that have ruled your 3-D experience until now.

The trick at this point is to replace the negative thought patterns with positive mental activity—the kind that will change your world, as well as the way you experience it.

Try the following exercise, if you like, as an interesting experiment in the reshaping of your reality: Pick an outcome that represents your biggest dream fulfilled. Pay no attention at all to the "reasons why not" that spring up immediately in response. You know the ones I mean. They're the very logical, rational stories your thinking mind relies upon to prevent you from attaining—or even, in many cases, attempting—that dream: *What do you mean, you want to open an ice cream factory? In this economy? You'd never find investors. Besides, you have a family to support. How would you pay the mortgage until the business became successful?*

"Reasons why not" are a perfectly normal part of the process; it's what the thinking mind does when you attempt to disrupt its comfortable patterns. But it's important to realize you have the power to choose whether or not to believe in those reasons. Mind mastery becomes your best friend in this, as deliberate conscious effort is required to override the cycle of negative thinking that has limited you in the past.

It's essential to develop the ability to overlook the "reasons why not." As you nourish and sustain that imagined outcome of your biggest dream fulfilled, guard especially against feelings of hopelessness, or helplessness, that may arise in response to "reasons why not;" beware the feeling of *I want to, but I can't.* Like it or not, this kind of mental activity is a clear request for failure.

Worrying about the barriers that seem to stand in the way of your fulfilled desire will automatically cause your inner creator-self to accept a desire for barriers as your actual request. Why? *Because your belief in barriers is much stronger than your belief in the fulfilled desire.* That's the way it works. Whichever outcome you feel and believe in most fully is the one you'll get.

IT'S NOW OR NEVER

As we know, all transformational work takes place only in the present. This is because past and future don't exist, of course. There is only the now.

The way to power up your consciously activated desires is to imagine them fulfilled in the present. (To imagine them fulfilled in the future is to want things that can only be experienced later, not now. Voila! Just as you requested, you'll be left in a perpetual state of unfulfilled desire, waiting for a tomorrow that never comes.)

So the idea is to get inside your fulfilled desire as completely as you can. Live it right now. If your dream is to sail around the world on your own yacht, it isn't enough to imagine seeing yourself on the yacht, as if you are merely looking at a snapshot of yourself onboard this craft. The fulfillment of desire can't be approached as an intellectual exercise.

Climb inside that scenario. Experience it. *Be on the yacht.* Look around; view the scene through your own eyes, as if you are present onboard at this very moment. Feel the salt spray on your face, the wind blowing against your body. This yacht is yours *right now.*

(Your mind is likely informing you all the while of the many reasons you can't afford or shouldn't have this yachting adventure. Smile fondly at your oh-so-predictable mental activity, and then ignore it completely. Good. Where were we? Ah yes…onboard your oceangoing craft, knee deep in saltwatery experience.)

Hold onto those present moment sensations in your mind, and add all the emotions you would feel if you were actually enjoying that yachting experience right now. Feel the exhilaration of being out on the water with no horizon in sight; the joy in contemplating the adventure that lies ahead; the gratitude as you realize how easy it is to make this formerly impossible LOA dream come true. Take delight in the pure satisfaction of finally owning your own beautiful sailing vessel, just like you always wanted.

Inhabit the fulfilled desire as completely as you can. Believe in it and strive to make it every bit as real as your current surroundings. Let go of all thoughts except the desire itself, making the scenario come alive until it feels completely natural and true. The more authentically you can feel the sensations and emotions of your fulfilled desire, the more powerfully realized the desired outcome will be.

To sum up the steps of deliberate manifestation:
- Activate a desire
- Feel its reality
- Live it in the present
- Fully enjoy the emotions associated with it
- Believe in it totally

This process never fails. As in *never*. As in one hundred percent effective predictability. Without mental resistance, in fact, it would work instantaneously and with full power.

This is the law of 3-D causation, and the law is the law is the law. It always works. It moves mountains, both literally and figuratively. Only our disordered thinking and inability to accept our own limitless power can cause this law to seemingly operate with mixed or less-than-ideal results.

• • •

So that's the Law of Attraction in a nutshell. Yes, we tend to use it to get stuff, or to alleviate pain. And there's absolutely nothing wrong with that. Yet there's much more to LOA than meets the eye. In my observation, this law of causation seems to make up the very building blocks of the dream itself. It is the process that facilitates the creation of the 3-D universe, and everything in it. More significantly, it also seems to facilitate the *dismantling* of the 3-D universe, and everything in it.

LOA is an intrinsic part of the mechanism used to heal our split minds and correct our vision. Our collective ego mind devised this law of manifestation as a means to create a 3-D dream universe, and Spirit is happy to help us use this same mechanism to unmake said universe.

Need an example? See if this scenario rings a bell: Let's say we catch ourselves unhappily wanting to make somebody else guilty instead of us. We recognize that our perception of guilt is faulty; we're not seeing this guy correctly. So we decide we want to overlook the perceived guilt and see him as he really is in truth.

We know the desired outcome of this corrected vision would be peace, and that's what we're after. So we imagine the essential perfection of the other guy, and look beyond the "reasons why not" to the best of our ability. We drop all intellectual beliefs and past knowledge of this person's alleged misdeeds, and feel only his present holiness and perfection. And as we feel the reality of that perfection, we experience the sense of peace that was our original desired outcome.

Is this not a description of forgiveness? And is it not also a description of the law of 3-D causation at work? Indeed, as with LOA, if we were able to perform a forgiveness exercise with all parts of our mind united, feeling another's innocence in a completely unconflicted way, the exercise would activate unlimited creative power within us. ACIM calls this present moment of mega-forgiveness "The Holy Instant," and says its power would be enough to immediately allow us to awaken permanently from the dream.

. . .

There's an old Buddhist parable about the mythical Kankucho bird: Each evening as the sun sets, it cries plaintively in the cold because it has no nest to keep it warm. All night long it cries, vowing to the heavens that if it can just survive the bitter cold of this night, it will build a nest when the sun comes up.

Yet when the sun's warming rays arrive at last, the Kankucho, exhausted by its traumatic night, is lulled to sleep. *I'll build a nest tomorrow*, it thinks drowsily as its eyes start to close. *Right now I really need to catch up on all the sleep I missed.*

And so it goes through life, crying night after night, and sleeping day after day.

For the first fifteen years of my Buddhist practice, I was a big-time Kankucho bird. Every time the crap hit the fan in my daily life, I revved up my Buddhist practice, using it to manifest miraculous outcomes that solved my emergency problems in beautiful, unpredictably creative ways.

But then when times were good and I wasn't in any specific pain, I lost that fire and my Buddhist practice became stale and habitual. Although I still went through the motions of correct daily practice, I was really just coasting. Sleeping in the warm sunshine, exhausted from the long night of drama and trauma.

I couldn't help but notice how alive I felt whenever my Buddhist practice was really cooking; even though I was suffering from the crisis of the moment, I felt my spiritual connection as a fresh, welcoming breeze blowing through my life. When I relaxed my passion for Buddhism, on the other hand, I tended to become unpleasantly aware of the swampy, stagnant stink rising off my comfortable life.

I really liked how vibrant and energized I felt when my practice was firing on all cylinders. Eventually I realized I was setting up unconscious crises over and over, expressly so I could experience breakthrough periods of butt-kicking Buddhist practice. Gradually it dawned on me I would never be free of these frequent painful dramas, as long as I refused to bring my Buddhist practice alive during good times as well as bad.

In my sixteenth year of practice, after a nonstop five-month stint of ongoing drama, I'd finally had enough. I was permanently finished with manufacturing unwanted crises as fuel for spiritual growth. I vowed I would practice every day with equal passion and sincerity, no matter what circumstances were occurring at the time. And with pinpoint laser focus, I informed the universe: No more drama was needed. From that moment onward, I gladly chose to receive all my spiritual lessons in a gently joyous way instead.

I kept that vow, to practice with sincerity every day of the year. And because I gratefully chose a new, more positive spiritual paradigm instead of a disruptively painful one, manufactured drama has become a very rare occurrence in my life.

Instead of the old days of desperate emergencies, the catalysts for spiritual lessons nowadays tend to be unimaginably wonderful opportunities that come my way, forcing me to grow beyond my limiting self-image in the process. Each time I manage to take that next step in faith and heal what needs to be healed, magnificent new possibilities are revealed.

Oh sure, the spiritual lessons can still be hard, sometimes.

And just like back in the old days of horrible crises, they often require lots of work. Yet given the choice between catastrophic meltdown and beautiful opportunities as the catalyst of choice, I'm glad I went with the beautiful opportunities.

•   •   •

It may not seem like it, but we're still on the subject of LOA.

In classic gently joyous fashion, I inked a deal a while back, to put on my first official workshop. The kind where people pay actual money to participate in a full-day presentation. Here it was at last—the dreaded "Eckhart Tolle on a stage" thing.

I knew this day would come, of course; Spirit is never wrong.

Yet knowing this didn't make it any easier. Having to let people look at me; having to tear up the memorized scripts and speak as the Spirit moved me—well, just add spiders, as the saying goes, and this circumstance would bundle up all my greatest fears into one squirmy package of pain.

I had agreed to stop resisting public interaction several months before this; I surrendered it all to Spirit at that time. Or so I thought. Yet a speaking gig in Sedona right after the big surrender had still been enormously difficult. And since then, being interviewed had actually gotten harder, not easier. I was sick with dread at the thought of delivering a full-day presentation.

This was not the focus I wanted to carry with me into that upcoming workshop. Obsessive shyness, self-hatred and ancient, tangled-up pain were not what I wanted its underlying energy to be about. Heavenly love and divine healing were my goals for that workshop—and if I wanted to be a conduit for such transmission, I knew I couldn't afford to be wrapped up in my own terrified self-torment instead.

Clearly it was time for some serious self-inquiry. I looked

inward and focused as closely as possible on my fear of public interaction; I was determined to find out, once and for all, what it was actually made of. To my surprise, I discovered it didn't just rear its head whenever I was about to speak publicly. I realized I felt small stabs of this same fear and self-hatred every time I had to leave the house and be seen by anyone. I'd spent my whole life unthinkingly accepting ridiculous self-taught lies about my own worth, and as it turned out, I willingly suffered for it many times a day.

I decided enough was enough.

For the first time, I truly wanted to be free of this mistaken belief system *more* than I wanted the comfort of hanging onto the old familiar pain. I was finally ready to release it—but how to do that?

When a belief system is so deep and persistent it forms your whole self-identity, it's impossible to imagine what you'd be without it. More to the point, when this belief system colors every aspect of your 3-D experience, where do you even begin the dismantling process? I started poking randomly at this big, amorphous blob of an issue by using more self-inquiry. What I found surprised me.

At the root of this mess was love. Or rather, lack of love. I knew I had never fully healed the lifelong unconscious belief that I was a poisonous mutant, filled with a murderous egoic filth that nobody else had. (It was a hell of a way to convince myself I was special, but that was how my ego mind had always operated. Nobody was as vile as me. Or as shameful as me.)

The truth is, we're all made of the exact same stuff, and it isn't vile or shameful. "Vile" and "shameful" are just mistaken thoughts we hold about ourselves. Yet that was largely an intellectual understanding, not something I authentically knew in my heart.

Through self-inquiry I became aware I believed I was incapable of the kind of love other people feel. According to my ego mind, I often went through the hollow motions of feeling love, but this was just an act; a cynical, predatory attempt to blend in and seem human. And in its darkest insinuations, my ego whispered that this inability to know love was also the reason I would never fully awaken from the dream of 3-D existence. Divine love was not something I could ever embody, because I was made of some other profane and loveless thing entirely.

Jackpot. These are the kinds of deeply mistaken thoughts that need darkness to survive. It seemed I'd found not only the answer to what lay beneath my fear of going public, but also the very root of my resistance when in the presence of Heaven's radiant light.

(Incidentally, I realized shortly after this that my food obsession—another big, amorphous issue with mysterious hidden roots—was part of the same mess. Food was not, as I'd always believed, my way of expressing love. Food was my *substitute* for love. I believed I was incapable of extending love; I also believed I was incapable of receiving it. My stunted, alien heart couldn't metabolize the nourishment that came from love, so I took what I could from food instead. Yikes.)

Using self-inquiry, I had identified the hidden nature of all these mistaken beliefs.

Now what?

I started to try a joining pool exercise, depositing the giant blob of mistaken belief at the water's edge. Suddenly Spirit intervened, gently erasing the scene before me and replacing it with a wordless inspiration to try LOA instead.

Really? LOA?

A surprising suggestion, but I agreed to give it a shot. Looking inward, I pictured my heart. I overlooked all my mistaken beliefs about it, all the "reasons why not," and imagined only my beautiful, unconflicted heart, functioning at full power. I watched as it began to radiate light and love, sending out wave upon wave of gentle illumination in all directions.

Next I added the venue of my upcoming workshop to this scene. I remained as before, streaming sweet, beautiful light, but now I was standing comfortably in front of a room full of workshop participants. I felt joy and tender friendship for each one of them. In my self-absorbed pain and fear, these attendees had been the "outlaw selves" I had refused to accept as my own. Yet now, in the clear heart-light of love, I could see them properly at last.

They were my perfect, eternal self.

I performed versions of this LOA exercise a number of times after that. As a result, things were changing on a very deep level, although I would've been hard-pressed at first to tell you exactly what those changes were.

I could sense it caused quite a lot of furniture rearrangement behind closed doors, so to speak. There was muffled bumping. How all this would impact my speaking engagements (or the rest of my life) was yet to be seen.

One thing is clear: LOA is a wonderful tool to use on those darkest, most persistent beliefs that resist dismantling by any other method.

Since it doesn't require us to understand all the parts of the problem first (beyond figuring out what the actual problem is, through means such as self-inquiry), LOA allows us to slip past the egoic gatekeeper and powerfully state our intention to embrace spiritual and emotional health *right now*.

I have no doubt there will be a certain amount of good old-fashioned joining and forgiveness and further self-inquiry needed, as all parts of an issue unravel and present themselves for healing. But LOA seems to get the ball rolling in a way that nothing else does.

•   •   •

There's one final point I'd like to make about LOA: I rarely use it these days (other than in the above sort of example) because it seems to require that we ourselves decide what we want to have/do/achieve/be, and then take steps to manifest that change.

The ego mind is firmly in charge of all such decisions and desires, so as a rule, I don't like to go there. I'd rather turn all my conflicts or perceived needs over to Spirit, and allow myself to be guided instead.

This is the way I resolved that dilemma, as I began using LOA to heal my heart: I was careful not to choose love *instead of* pain and fear. I didn't want to make that judgment call. I didn't want to define good versus bad, or create stories about choosing light and vanquishing dark. Instead of letting my own ego mind decide these things, I brought Spirit into the exercise with me. In short, I didn't come up with an egoic goal (*I want to be a great workshop presenter!*), I just indicated I was ready to release the blocks to love. I focused wordlessly on visualizing my own radiant, loving heart, but I was content to let Spirit take my newfound willingness and run with it.

And the rest of it was none of my business, really.

POSTSCRIPT: LORD WILLING
(AND THE CREEK DON'T RISE)

Well a few months have come and gone, since I first tried that powerful LOA exercise in which I visualized my own radiant, healthy heart. The changes stemming from that experience were subtle at first, and took awhile to register.

Within a few weeks, I began to realize I felt comfortable at last in my own skin. For the first time in my life I was now able to go out in public without any twinge of shame, or fear of being seen. And that was huge.

The forgiveness accompanying this LOA exercise—the authentic recognition that workshop attendees were truly my perfect, eternal self (rather than merciless judges)—seemed to have healed the half-century of pointless pain I'd felt over my physical appearance.

Yet as the workshop approached, I found I was still fearful about my public speaking abilities, and felt compelled to keep my comments tightly scripted. I just couldn't surrender enough to relax and let Spirit flow through me.

So I over-prepared, building a carefully crafted presentation on a thick stack of bullet point notes. And this did make me feel somewhat better about the whole prospect of speaking publicly. (Truthfully, I'd have loved to stand at a podium and read a speech off a teleprompter for eight hours, but in a pinch, meticulously prepared bullet points would have to do.)

I knew this canned presentation was not what was being asked of me; how could Spirit be free to do its work through me, if I refused to let it in? God knows, I'd been trying to let go for months. Years. But I couldn't seem to stop prefabricating every moment of the presentation, squeezing out all possibility of spontaneity. My need to protect myself from error (and judgment) was just too great. Every minute of our time together would be filled, leaving no room even for questions and answers at the end.

The workshop was scheduled to take place in Baton Rouge, Louisiana on May 21, 2011. Which, as it turned out, was also the projected date of Judgment Day. Yep, *that* Judgment Day. I made plenty of jokes beforehand, but I was secretly a little uneasy about the date's "end times" significance.

It's not that I believed in the Rapture story; it was just that I had noticed a pattern of highly disruptive events seemed to follow every time I tried to plan a speaking engagement. My own terrified resistance to public speaking seemed to reflect my hysteria back at me on the bigscreen, writ large in the form of external turmoil of all kinds.

For example, the co-presenter of a workshop I'd planned for September of 2010 bowed out due to terminal illness—and then the workshop venue itself, a beautiful little Victorian church, abruptly closed its doors and became a bed and breakfast instead.

Okaaay.

Shortly after that workshop was cancelled, I was invited to speak at a Unity Church in Sedona. I had a wonderful phone conversation with the church's minister; we seemed to have a lot in common and he was very supportive.

Then a week or so before the event, I learned the guy had abruptly resigned his ministry, taking his assistant with him. Nobody was in charge of the church's event schedule anymore, I was told, but I could still come and speak if I wanted to.

I kept the date. As we made our way to the church that evening, the heavens opened without warning, pummeling the town with hail and rain. And then as quickly as it appeared, the storm cleared completely. It had done the job it was intended to do: It kept all but the diehard listeners from coming out to hear me speak.

(As I describe these events, do you find yourself thinking *Oh Carrie, sometimes storms and upheavals just happen—it isn't always about you?* Ah, but it is. I'm an endlessly powerful unconscious creator, after all. Just like you.)

Anyway, the hysteria surrounding this Rapture business fit in perfectly with that pattern of disruption. And as the date of the workshop drew closer, another potential disaster loomed: Due to record flooding elsewhere in the region, the Mississippi had been threatening to breach its levees in Louisiana. Funnily enough, the river was predicted to crest in Baton Rouge on the same day as my workshop.* Would floods prevent people from being able to attend? And if so, what was next—locusts?

•   •   •

My friend Steve and I caught a plane from California the morning before the workshop. The flight would include a short layover in Dallas before landing in Baton Rouge around dinnertime. Plenty of time to get settled at the hotel and run through my bullet point notes again, before hitting the hay.

Well. After an unscheduled stop in Abilene, we landed in Dallas a few hours later than planned, to discover all connecting flights had been cancelled due to weather. We looked out the window—it was sunny and clear.

*The Army Corps of Engineers stepped in a few days prior to the crest, alleviating the situation before the river was allowed to reach the flood stage.

We considered our options: We could find a hotel in Dallas and try again the following morning (which would get us into Baton Rouge around noon. Not so good; the workshop was supposed to start at nine-thirty.) We could turn around and go back home. Or we could rent a car and drive. The flight from Dallas to Baton Rouge would have lasted only an hour and ten minutes; by my calculations that meant approximately a six hour drive. That would put us in Baton Rouge at one o'clock in the morning.

I had no idea what I was supposed to do, so I gave up trying to figure it out. I handed it over to Spirit and got out of the way. Immediately I was flooded with a deeply pervasive sense of wellbeing, and the wordless answer came: *Road trip.*
(Or more accurately, the answer was: *Whatever you decide, it's perfect.* I then chose the road trip, and knew it was all good, no matter the outcome.)

I bought some airport snacks to tide us over, and within minutes we found ourselves on a bus headed for the rental car offices. Fat raindrops began to fall as we entered the facility.

Apparently we were not the first to think of this transportation solution—several flights before ours had been cancelled. The place was loaded with stranded passengers urgently trying to make other arrangements. With perfectly detached serenity, we somehow managed to obtain the last available one-way rental car in all of Dallas/Fort Worth International Airport. And it came equipped with a GPS unit, to boot. Snacks, satellite navigation— what more could we want?

Well, I suppose we could've wanted our suitcase. It had been checked through to Baton Rouge, and we'd been unable to untangle the mystery of its current whereabouts; it could've been loaded onto a couple of different planes, neither of which had apparently left the ground.

Oh well. No matter.

It was eight o'clock and raining hard, yet we felt oddly peaceful and utterly free as we headed out of Dallas in our comfortable rental car. Spirit was in charge of the journey; Steve and I were just along for the ride.

Flights had been cancelled with very good reason, as it turned out. Rain pounded with startling force, the torrential blackness interrupted only by savage, sideways lightning forks that lit our surroundings brighter than daylight.

The drive took ten hours; the storm lasted unbroken for the first eight. Through it all, we felt ourselves suspended within an extraordinary sense of present-moment acceptance, wellbeing and peace.

We arrived in Baton Rouge at six o'clock in the morning. Word had gone out to workshop attendees (some of whom were driving several hours to be there) that the presentation would be starting a bit late. This gave us time to check into our respective rooms, shower and reconvene for breakfast before making our way to the workshop venue.

Steve and I arrived at ten o'clock, ready to go—not so bad; just a half hour late—to learn that a handful of people were still on the road and wouldn't hit town for another hour.

No problem. We could wait.

At eleven o'clock, as I faced a roomful of smiling people, I was wearing my mildly sticky travel clothes from the day before, and no makeup. I'd had no sleep. And our workshop would now be an hour and a half shorter than I'd planned for.

And I laughed. Delightedly. Throwing my carefully rehearsed presentation out the window, I peacefully let Spirit take over.

And everything was perfect, exactly as it was.

Simply do this:
Be still,
and lay aside all thoughts of what you are and what God is;
all concepts you have learned about the world;
all images you hold about yourself.

Empty your mind of everything it thinks is either true or false,
or good or bad;
of every thought it judges worthy,
and all the ideas of which it is ashamed.
Hold onto nothing.

~ A Course in Miracles

Following is an afterchat with Nouk Sanchez, co-author of *Take Me to Truth – Undoing the Ego*. (A proper afterword seemed way too stuffy for a book like this one.) It's a conversation about the importance of surrender.

Just to be clear: As we examine our chosen topic of surrender, it's obvious we're surrendering *to* something. In this discussion, we sometimes choose to call that something "God." Yet we're not really talking about a separate deity, a Big Daddy in the Sky. We're talking about our One eternal self, the all-loving creator of everything that is, was or ever will be.

THE MIRACLE OF SURRENDER

CARRIE: I'm calling this discussion *The Miracle of Surrender* because it's a miracle anybody ever manages to do it. The impulse to surrender one's own free will to a higher power does not exactly come naturally to the average human being; it certainly didn't for me.

Even a few short years ago, I was dreadfully reluctant to surrender to Spirit because I was convinced surrender equaled suffering. I went totally Old Testament in my assumptions about it: I thought surrender meant I'd be asked to chop my child in half or something. Or maybe I'd be told to wander around starving in the desert for a few decades. Bible stories seemed full of such seemingly capricious demands.

Now I shake my head and laugh at my mistaken belief. As usual, I had it completely backwards. Not only doesn't it bring suffering—surrender brings surefire guaranteed peace. And not only peace, but authentic healing and beautiful, clever win-win solutions to 3-D dilemmas I never could've solved on my own.

Thank God for surrender! It's gotten my ass out of a jam more times than I can count.

NOUK: Yes, the "surrender" word has gotten such an incredibly bad rap. Like you, I spent much of my life equating surrender with loss, sacrifice and suffering. The word itself is often misinterpreted to mean giving up something valuable, which is crazy. The only thing I gave up through surrender is suffering—and that's hardly something valuable!

CARRIE: It's pretty startling when you suddenly realize what you're "giving up" through surrender is completely worthless—not only worthless but grossly undesirable—and what you're getting in exchange is everything you've ever wanted or prayed for. It's a hell of a realization. And it seems so obvious, once you finally recognize it.

NOUK: Here's something else that's crazy: Our so-called "free will." I've come to recognize individual freedom is purely *the free will to choose to suffer*. It's the will to choose a path other than consistent love, joy and peace. And truly, who in their right mind wants that? God's will (our One true self) is the ultimate in *real* free will.

CARRIE: Ah yes. The big GW. God's will is a tough one for us stubborn humans to accept—we who invest so much in the idea of individual freedom and autonomy. Yet, as you point out, God's will *is the same thing* as our own true will; it just doesn't seem that way to us at the moment.

So, Nouk, what was the key for you, in helping you realize that surrender is the opposite of suffering? What changed to help you surrender more deeply into Spirit? (For this conversation, I'll use the words "Spirit" and "God" interchangeably, if you don't mind.)

NOUK: First I had to take a good long look at what I believed about the nature and will of God. Did I really believe God's will is total love, and nothing else?

I came to realize I didn't trust God's love and that's why I was terrified of surrender. Like someone said to me only yesterday, *"What if God wants to teach me a few lessons? What if trusting God turns out to be far worse than trusting my own (ego) self?"*

CARRIE: Well there's that Old Testament misperception showing up again. I guess a lot of us have it. The idea of a vengeful God is woven so deeply into our psyches.

NOUK: Yes, and that misperception is responsible for so much of our suffering. We perceive God through our ego. So the God we're terrified of, is one we think has an even bigger ego than ours. This God comes complete with judgment, guilt, punishment, lessons through suffering, sacrifice—oh, and I nearly forgot...the need to "earn" his love.

CARRIE: Yeah. We're told (by ACIM) that no punishment awaits us when we return our awareness to the One loving self. But how can an ego mind believe that? We ourselves would punish a similar transgressor until hell froze. Maybe longer. We're awfully good at holding grudges, so it's natural for us to assume our creator would behave the same way. And of course our creator would also be every bit as petty as we are. So it only makes sense to suck up and curry favor if we want to stay on God's good side.

NOUK: What a laugh! God (not the one we project, but the real creator) is only love, pure love. This is who we really are, beneath the personal "me" that insists on perceiving the 3-D world through a lens of fear, deprivation and separation.

For a long time, I was living a contradiction. On the surface I believed God was love. Love with no opposite. But still, my everyday experience was based on deep belief in deprivation and scarcity. So while I *said* I believed God was love with no opposite, my actual experience was anything but that.

For me, the breakthrough occurred when I finally made the connection: God really is all-encompassing love, *which has no opposite.* Well, if that's true…then what the hell is everything else? Disease, scarcity, pain, emotional suffering, loss and death—ah, hello? Either God is all, or suffering is all. Only one is real. Which one?

CARRIE: Well it's choosing once again between "right" and "happy," isn't it? And we can't have both, because each cancels out the other.

NOUK: Yes, that's it. We are all so damned hypnotized into believing and accepting that two diametrically opposed realities can co-exist. Well, sorry, that's not possible; only one is real. Love is all. The ego is nothing.

If you believe a second reality made of anything other than love can co-exist alongside the reality of total love, you've lost your connection with the One true self. So this was one heck of an epiphany for me! Finally recognizing divine love and suffering were mutually exclusive, helped me choose definitively between the two. And then I leapt wholeheartedly into surrendering everything that was *not* of God's love.

CARRIE: Recently I had a very powerful surrender experience: I was deep in meditation, and feeling gratitude for Kurt's presence as he accompanies me through this 3-D life; coupled with that gratitude was the solemn (and somewhat ashamed) realization of how much ego bullshit I pile onto my image of who he is. So I was suddenly inspired to perceive him clearly, without all the ego interpretation.

I attempt this sort of thing all the time, but usually my ego mind is quick to point out that it's too powerful to allow such a thing. It reminds me I will need years more hard work before I'm strong enough to overlook the unfathomable power of my own egoic perception. And usually I fully agree with it.

But this time something changed. I surrendered all my misperceptions about Kurt to Spirit, and as I did so, I became flooded with extra strength and sanity. And with that sanity I clearly perceived firsthand that my ego only has the power to block true perception because I allow it.

So I decided to stop allowing it. I surrendered belief in my ego's power to block truth. And as I stopped believing wholeheartedly in its strength, I could feel my ego's usual power of resistance diminishing rapidly.

All of this was touch and go; the changes weren't permanent. My ego mind kept tossing me stories of judgment and limitation throughout this surrender process, hoping one would stick. I viewed each of these stories through the clear lens of Spirit's "eyeglasses," and with this corrected vision I was able to allow each story to pass me by without buying into it.

Each ego story was a fresh choice; at any time I could've changed my mind and chosen the ego's interpretation of Kurt's reality instead. Or I could've chosen to believe I'm not ready and not capable of choosing against the power of my own ego.

(Both these storylines remained active throughout the meditation.) But I was able to surrender each story to Spirit for reinterpretation and healing.

NOUK: The power of choice is crucial in undoing the ego.

CARRIE: Yes, I agree the power of choice is key. Or rather, *realizing* we have the power of choice. That's a big one. Everything else seems to fall into place once we start to authentically realize who's actually in charge.

Anyway, it was a gorgeous meditation; it went on for hours. I've felt quite different ever since it happened.

NOUK: Well, that was a pretty miraculous shift, Carrie! I like that your surrender experience came gently, and not through great suffering.

All my most valuable leaps forward in surrender came from reaching an unbearable limit in emotional suffering. Only recently have I pledged to make future leaps through joy, instead of pain. But of course, that means being prepared to accept whatever lessons I've asked for—and sooner, rather than later. Resistance always prolongs suffering.

CARRIE: Gently joyous, baby. Definitely the way to go! But you're right—in asking for lessons to come in gently joyous packages, it means we agree to pay attention to the lesson and embrace it now as a catalyst for learning, rather than waiting for something unbearably painful to force us to stop and learn the same lesson some other time.

Anyway, Nouk, now that I've described my recent breakthrough in surrender, can you share an example of your own?

NOUK: Well, the following surrender example occurred before I'd learned about gently joyous means. It was in Australia with my husband Nick, in 2004. We were going through a challenging time; my mother had just passed, and my daughter Rikki was ill. But they were not the seat of my perceived problem. Nick was.

On top of being completely uninterested in spiritual awakening, he was also undergoing an unsuccessful job search in Australia. And he was groping in the dark, trying to find a way to fit in within a new culture (Nick is a US citizen).

Our relationship became terribly strained. So much so, that I felt suicidal. And I saw the "cause" as Nick's cantankerous behavior. I was utterly defeated, and despaired that I would never awaken from suffering. *After all I've learned through ACIM*, I thought, *how could this terrible alienation be occurring between us?*

When I couldn't take it anymore, I finally surrendered. I sat crying and gave all my grievances to Spirit, including my recognition that I did not understand anything. I gave over my blaming Nick, as well. It was an instant of true surrender. I guess it was a moment where I willingly retracted all of my ego perception. And by leaving a "gap" and not needing to fill it, there came a holy instant of acceptance.

Then, into that holy instant, came the most surprising thing:

THERE IS NO NICK! I heard this booming from an inner voice. I was stunned.

"What do you mean, there is *no Nick*?? So who, then, is the cause of all this conflict in our relationship if there is no Nick?"

And that was it! That was the moment I recognized there is only me, only my own projections that I perceived in another person. This epiphany was monumental. It changed my life. And from that moment onward, Nick and I never had another conflict. Like you with Kurt, I perceived Nick as he really was: Absolute perfect love. The immense gratitude I have for him is undeniable. I "see" him now! And that's all any of us really wants—to be "seen" as our perfect, innocent self.

A miracle occurred that day, seven years ago. I never said a word to Nick about what happened. Yet his perception was totally transformed along with mine. And because I "saw" him, he now "sees" me.

CARRIE: How inspiring this is. Thank you for sharing. And I know what you mean, when you say you never spoke a word about it with Nick. No words are necessary, when that kind of miraculous shift occurs. It seems everyone shares equally in the healing, and nothing ever needs to be said about it.

There's one more surrender-related topic I'd like to explore— one final argument, I guess, for giving surrender a try: The comparative efficiency of problem-solving through the ego, versus surrender to Spirit.

Our ego minds are in charge when we try to change or fix aspects of our 3-D lives, so the outcome is always bound to be less than ideal. Ego minds never perceive the "problem" correctly, so the "solution" will be flawed at best. Besides, ego minds aren't loving by nature, and they never know what's best for anybody. On top of it all, egos are designed to seek happiness, but never actually find it.

Objectively speaking, when we take all of this evidence into account as we weigh the value of relying on our egos, we have to admit they're pretty crummy tools for fixing what ails us.

Yet I find when anything is surrendered to Spirit (whether it's a 3-D world issue, or a misperception about another person's perfection), the resolution is always gentle, always loving, and always win-win. Everybody concerned is genuinely happier and more free because I allowed Spirit—my highest self—to handle it for me. Who wouldn't want to ask for such wonderfully effective help, instead of insisting on screwing it up alone?

NOUK: I agree, surrendering our concerns brings about the most awesome outcomes. I see it time and again, and am totally gob-smacked at the win-win perfection of all that I've given over to Spirit.

Why would I ever again want to control anything, and wind up with the usual botched-up scenario that the ego is notorious for?

I am still learning how to surrender pain and fear. Now I summon the balls to say "no!" whenever I'm tempted to believe pain and fear are real, and that I need to defend myself against them. I choose to remember there's only One truth, the truth of God's love, which has no opposite. And I surrender everything that is not of this all-encompassing love.

If only I had known about this piece of the awakening puzzle before, I would have saved myself twenty years of unnecessary suffering. I guess I had to experience the road of many mistakes in order to finally get it.

And now? Gently joyous is the way home!

CARRIE: Amen, sister.

ALSO BY CARRIE TRIFFET

LONG TIME NO SEE: Diaries of an Unlikely Messenger

a rip-snorting spiritual memoir

"**Long Time No See clearly illuminates the principles of A Course in Miracles** as they apply to everyday life... Did I mention it's also funny as hell?" -- *Gary Renard, author of The Disappearance of the Universe*

"**We love this book!**...Carrie Triffet demonstrates how life is meant to be lived as a co-creator with God." -- *Nouk Sanchez & Tomas Vieira, Co-authors of Take Me to Truth; Undoing the Ego*

"**Written with fresh, oddball sensibility,** this is soulful self-realization at its finest." -- *Sequoia Hamilton, editor-in-chief, Awaken Journal*

★ ★ ★ ★ ★

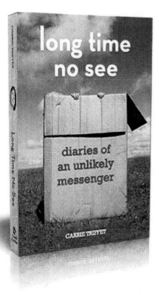

Long Time No See traces Carrie Triffet's unlikely journey through 20 years of Buddhist practice, to a wholly unexpected awakening in 2005 that changes everything. This book also contains *The Crash Course*, a brief, irreverent, yet highly accurate synopsis of *A Course in Miracles*.

For more about *Long Time No See* (or to download a free copy of *The Crash Course*) visit
www.unlikelymessenger.com

Long Time No See is the 2010 winner of the Independent Publisher Book Award